Our Lives Are Not Our Own
Saying "Yes" to God

Rochelle Melander
and Harold Eppley

Augsburg Fortress

Minneapolis

OUR LIVES ARE NOT OUR OWN
Saying "Yes" to God

Direct Scripture quotations are from New Revised Standard Version Bible, copyright © 1989 Division of Christian Education of the National Council of the Churches of Christ in the United States of America. Used by permission.

Editor: Carol Throntveit

Cover Design: Koechel Peterson and Associates, Inc., Minneapolis, MN
                www.koechelpeterson.com

Cover photo: Koechel Peterson and Associates, Inc.

ISBN 0-8066-4999-2

The paper used in this publication meets the minimum requirements of American National Standard for Information Sciences—Permanence of Paper for Printed Library Materials, ANSI Z329.48-1984.

Contents

Acknowledgments

Over and over God shows us that our writing is not our own! We thank God for richly blessing us with new projects that enrich our lives and our work.

We thank the people who stepped up to do emergency childcare in the past months: Diane and Dick Melander, Kate Rogers and her family, Gretchen Yoder-Froh, and Kim Garski.

We thank the people who hold us accountable by sharing ideas and inklings, especially Tim Pearson, Carol Gerrish, Donnita Moeller, Laurie and Paul Stumme-Diers, Sarah and Paul Lutter, Aleta Norris, Jan Veseth-Rogers and many others!

Finally, we thank our children, Samuel and Eliana, who by their very presence have called us to be accountable.

Introduction: Staying on Task

Our son Sam likes to daydream. Because of this, he tells us, he has trouble staying on task. In first grade, especially at the German immersion school that Sam attends and where he is required to work in German, staying on task is essential. Those who are able to stay on task learn to read and write and complete their assignments on time. Those who do not stay on task receive a second opportunity to experience first grade. And so we spend many of our supper hours talking about accountability. What does "stay on task" mean? Why might that be important? What benefit might Sam receive from staying on task (besides being promoted to second grade)?

We are both Lutheran clergy who, like other Lutherans, have been frustrated by the uncomfortable mix of grace and accountability. How do Lutherans say "Yes" to God *through our actions* when we believe that, at least when it comes to salvation, it is only God who can say "Yes" to us? We are saved by grace through faith alone, not by our works or our decision to follow Jesus. When does our "Yes" look like works-righteousness instead of accountability to God and others? Theologically, it gets sticky!

Claimed by God's grace

The theological gift we offer as Lutherans is our indefatigable insistence on grace. We believe that even our *ability to believe* that Jesus' death and resurrection was given *for us* comes from God. We do not decide. We do not choose. God does.

In this grace-centered theological climate, speaking about accountability can be challenging; it too easily begins to focus on what we do—our "works." Some quote James—"So faith, by itself, if it has no works, is dead" (James 2:17). Some talk about works as a part of sanctification, the process of the Holy Spirit working within the Christian. For most of us, any conversation about works is fraught

5

with danger. It can easily become a conversation about *working* toward salvation—and thus dismissed as "works-righteousness."

Because of this, we Lutherans rarely engage in conversations of Christian accountability or how our lives reflect God's amazing grace. And when we do, we often slip off the road into the ditches of guilt and fear.

Claimed by guilt

Guilt motivates. As church and community members, guilt is often the prime motivation for working for the realm of God. We hear things like, "You should serve the church. If you don't serve, no one will. Then the church will fall apart. And it can't fall apart because people need the church. And if they need the church and we're not here, it will be all your fault, because you didn't volunteer."

From bishop and synod staff to pastor, from pastor to parishioner, and from parishioner to parishioner, guilt is used as a tool to encourage service in the church. Unfortunately, volunteers recruited by guilt are generally not happy givers. They often feel anger and resentment toward those who have manipulated them with guilt. That resentment then bleeds into their feelings for the church and sometimes for God. Volunteers who have been motivated by guilt may leave the church for a healthier environment. They also may choose to use the same guilt-ridden tactics on other members. Works motivated by guilt create a vicious, unhealthy cycle in the church.

Scared straight

Fear motivates. As children—and even as adults—many of us have been terrified into accountability. Television preachers and popular Christian speakers capitalize on our fear of death, preaching to us about the judgment to come. They promise that our good works and right attitudes will be our tickets to heaven, while our acts of rebellion will send us straight to hell. No matter our final destination, the choice belongs to us: We have the power to decide where we will spend eternity.

Despite their theological education and training, even Lutheran pastors sometimes allow a theology of fear to intrude in their preaching, if only through a lack of clarity. But even if average Lutherans don't get it from their clergy, it's out there; it's part of our popular cultural ethic to believe that we are rewarded or punished on the basis of our actions. It's not surprising then, that many view God as an angry and vengeful judge who will give us only what we rightly deserve.

In the long run, fear is not the best motivator for Christian accountability. When we relate to God only as one who is "out to get us," we lose sight of the "immeasurable riches of (God's) grace" (Ephesians 2:7). We find ourselves tiptoeing through life, obsessed with taking a misstep instead of allowing our lives to be the joyful, liberated dance God wants them to be.

Secular salvation

The popular culture values and venerates people who are accountable with their lives. School children often have community service requirements in addition to their academic responsibilities. Children, youth, and adults are encouraged to give back through activities like collecting teddy bears for homeless children or nonperishable foodstuffs for local food banks, working in "soup kitchens," volunteering for community cleanup, and so forth—and applauded for it when they do. Oprah Winfrey gives out "Use Your Life" awards, encouraging people to share their gifts for the good of humanity. Our society makes heroes of those who give their time and money to the good of other people.

None of this is bad. In fact, it's great! Yet as Christians, we long for our conversations about doing good to be connected to what God has first done for us. We want our conversations about using our lives to be centered in our devotion to Jesus. How can we connect the dots in such a way that we are faithful to both the biblical call to service and a grace-centered theology?

Hungering and thirsting for God

Saint Paul wrote, "And whatever you do, in word or deed, do everything in the name of our Lord Jesus, giving thanks to God . . . " (Colossians 3:17). We long for the whole of our lives to be claimed by God's grace. We long to know that our lives have a purpose, that the world is better because of our actions and presence. We want to know how what we do with our time, abilities, and resources relates to our calling as children of God. Jesus said, "You did not choose me but I chose you. And I appointed you to go and bear fruit, fruit that will last, so that the Father will give you whatever you ask him in my name" (John 15:16). We want to know that our lives bear fruit and bear some resemblance to the God who chooses us.

As Christians and as pastors we, too, have been searching for a place to speak meaningfully about how our lives can reflect the amazing grace of God. When we have no place to go for conversation, we write. That is how we work out the tenets of the faith for ourselves. When this opportunity to write about accountability appeared, we jumped for joy! Finally! A chance to talk with Lutherans about being accountable as Lutherans.

How to use this book

We think of this book as the beginning of a dialogue. It is not a theological treatise, though we speak about God. It is not a Bible study, though we reference the Bible. It is not a "how-to" manual, though we tell stories about how some Christians are being accountable.

The book is divided into topical chapters. Each chapter contains several essays about the topic at hand. A list of questions, suitable for group discussion, appears at the end of each chapter. They are provided only as suggestions for your dialogue. Feel free to add your own questions to the mix. The resource list provides further direction for those who are interested in getting help to change the shape of their daily lives.

Who can use this book?

This book can be used individually or as a group. As a "dialogue starter" on issues such as accountability, stewardship, community, grace, and response, we believe it is best used with a group. Here are some groups that might benefit from the book:

- Families
- Bible study groups
- Small groups gathered for book or topical study
- Youth groups
- Confirmation classes
- Stewardship planning and/or discussion groups
- Adult education classes
- Community groups
- Church staffs
- Camp and retreat ministries
- Clergy groups

A free ride

Watching "Mister Roger's Neighborhood" one morning, we heard Mr. McFeeley say something like, "We certainly live wonderful lives. It's a free ride every day." He's right. Each day comes to us as a complete gift from God. What we make of it is our gift back to God. We give you this book as an opportunity to make your "free ride" a glorious opportunity to give thanks and praise to God!

Blessings on your conversations,
Rochelle Melander
Harold Eppley

1

Our Lives Are Not Our Own

In a world where we all make many choices every day, there remain three essential matters that none of us can do anything to change: We were born, we will die, and no matter what course our lives take, God will always love us.

God's love for us becomes most apparent in our Baptism. In that moment we are born again, we die to sin, and we are raised with Christ to new life. Thus, our Baptism brings together those three essential matters—birth, death, and God's love, and sets the course for every future choice we will make. St. Paul reminds us that "as many of you as were baptized into Christ have clothed yourselves with Christ" (Galatians 3:27). We belong to Christ. Our lives are not our own.

Christian accountability is about the choices *we* make—choices that by virtue of our Baptism involve not only ourselves, but also the God who refuses to stop loving us and the community of faith, that family into which we have been born again.

— Saying "Yes" to God —

For the Son of God, Jesus Christ, whom we proclaimed among you, Silvanus and Timothy and I, was not "Yes and No"; but in him it is always "Yes." For in him every one of God's promises is a "Yes." For this reason it is through him that we say the "Amen," to the glory of God.

  2 Corinthians 1:19-20

They know that this is a holy moment in their lives. They know that they are supposed to be thinking about their relationship with Jesus and the promises that they are about to make. Yet despite the seriousness with which they approach this moment, they can't keep their minds totally focused on the task at hand.

As they stand before the pastor and stare at the cross on the altar, unwanted thoughts keep popping into their heads: "Am I sweating? Does my hair look all right? Will that zit on my chin show up in the photos? What if I forget my lines? Or my voice squeaks? I hope I don't pass out or throw up."

Yet despite the anxiety, this is a holy moment. With trembling voices and thumping hearts, they answer the pastor's questions from the "Service for Affirmation of Baptism" in the *Lutheran Book of Worship* (p. 199-200):

"Do you renounce all the forces of evil, the devil, and all his empty promises?"

"I do," the confirmands reply in unison. Yes!

"Do you believe in God the Father?"

"I believe in God the Father Almighty . . . ," they reply, remembering to hold up their heads, trying to keep pace with the others, and inwardly praying that they won't forget these words they have committed to memory.

Yes! I believe in God.

Yes! I believe in Jesus.

Yes! I believe in the Holy Spirit.

Their parents beam. Their confirmation teacher smiles. And all the congregation stands with them and prays for them.

Then come the questions that each of the confirmands must answer in turn. This is the difficult part. Sure, they just confessed their faith in the words of the Apostles' Creed, but they were speaking those words in unison. If some of them forgot a few words or mispronounced "Pontius Pilate," it was no big deal. The rest of the group would cover for them. Now they must speak for themselves. Now they will make that promise for which God will hold them accountable for the rest of their lives. This is serious business!

"Do you intend," asks the pastor, "to continue in the covenant God made with you in Holy Baptism . . . ?" (See *LBW*, p. 201.)

If ever there was a time to pass out, it would be now. If ever there was a time to bolt for the door, this would be it. Yet each confirmand, with a sense of confidence that can come only from God, speaks his or her part in turn. "I do, and I ask God to help and guide me," each one answers, paraphrasing those words once spoken by a man who cried out before Jesus, "I believe; help my unbelief" (Mark 9:24)!

Yes, God, I believe and yes, God, I will serve you, but only if you help me. When we are confirmed, we affirm that our lives are not our own. We remember that when we were baptized, God claimed us as God's very own children: we were "sealed by the Holy Spirit and marked with the cross of Christ forever." When we were baptized, God said "Yes" to us, an affirmation that resounds through every moment of our lives, in this world and the next.

In confirmation, we say "Yes" to God. We respond affirmatively to the covenant, to the never-failing promise God makes to us in Baptism. The promises we make when we are confirmed ("to live among God's faithful people; to hear God's Word and share in the Lord's Supper; to proclaim the good news of God in Christ through word and deed; to serve all people, following the example of our Lord Jesus; and to strive for justice and peace in all the world" *LBW,*

p. 201) center on the two relationships that were established when we were baptized. In Baptism, we entered into an eternal relationship with God, while also being joined to the church, the body of Christ, thereby beginning a lifelong relationship in the community of believers (1 Corinthians 12:13). Note the passive tense of these sentences. It is not the baptized person who chooses the relationship with God and the church. God always does the choosing. As Jesus said in John's Gospel, "You did not choose me but I chose you" (John 15:16a).

And so we need not only God's help to lead accountable Christian lives, we also need the support of our faith community. Therefore, the newly baptized are often welcomed with these words: "We receive you as fellow members of the body of Christ, children of the same heavenly Father, and workers with us in the kingdom of God."

"Yes," says the faith community to the newly baptized. Yes, we are one with you in Christ. We're all in this together. As we welcome you, we promise to be accountable to each other as members of the community of faith.

⤙ The Pressure Is Off ⤚

For there is no distinction, since all have sinned and fall short of the glory of God; they are now justified by his grace as a gift, through the redemption that is in Christ Jesus.

⤚ *Romans 3:22b-24*

As children, we both loved playing Chutes and Ladders™. The object of the game was to reach the winner's square at the top of the board. To succeed, one had to land more often on the ladders, illustrated by good deeds that moved the players up the board toward success. The successful player had to avoid the chutes, illustrated by small sins and catastrophes (such as breaking dishes or eating forbidden cookies) that sent the player flying back toward the beginning.

Though a part of us longed to experience the fun of flying down the chute, we knew that success was achieved by avoiding the chutes. For many, Chutes and Ladders™ is an apt metaphor for accountability in life: We hold our destinies in our hands. We can choose salvation or damnation. And one little mistake could wreck it all. Despite our greatest efforts to be good, to follow God, to get to the top—we might break a dish, eat too many cookies, or fail to help a friend. We might sin. And then, whoosh! Back to square one.

In Lutheran theology, God wreaks havoc on the Chutes and Ladders™ metaphor. We can't get to the top by avoiding the chutes of life. And, we aren't doomed to hit the bottom if we happen to fall into one (which we will!). Grace catches us and breaks our fall. God comes down the ladder. Good deeds or not, God comes down—to us and for us. Extrapolating on an image of the apostle Paul in Romans 8:19-21, we might compare our relationship with God through Christ to receiving a "Get Out of Jail Free" card in Monopoly™.

In Jesus' birth, God became one of us—"coming down" from heaven and joining us in life on earth. Jesus died a horrible death and was raised from the dead for us and for our salvation. Our good deeds do not bring us to the top of the ladder, earning us salvation. God saves us by grace alone. Even our faith in Jesus comes to us as a free gift. Nothing we do or decide can earn our salvation. Our bad deeds do not topple us from our home in God's realm. In fact, when chutes appear and we tumble down them, God is with us both on the way down and at the bottom, catching us when we fall. Lutheran theology recognizes that we all fall down. We cannot get up on our own strength of character or through our good deeds. God both lifts us up and carries us.

It is God's saving act in Jesus that frees us from the power of sin, death, and the need to earn God's favor. We no longer need to work or worry over our salvation. We know that as beloved children of God, we are also a part of the community of faith, God's realm here on earth. We belong to God and God's people. God is with us now and will be with us when we die. In this life and the next, we belong to God.

But God's saving act in Jesus does more than free us *from* the bondage of sin. God's act frees us *for* service to God, the community of faith, and the world. In loving gratitude to God for all that God has done for us, we live accountable both to God and to one another.

In a sense, because we no longer have to worry about our status in the realm of God—we are free to act boldly *for* the welfare of others. The "pressure" is off. The outcome has been decided. We don't have to worry that our actions or missteps will somehow lose us the keys to the kingdom. What we do with our lives says "thank you" to God; it's our gift back to God for all that God has done for us. We have been made free by God, and in that gracious state we can use all that God has given us to act on behalf of others and the world. We are to be the words and hands of Jesus to those we meet each day.

⟶ What We Do Matters ⟵

Should we continue to sin in order that grace may abound? By no means!

⟶ Romans 6:1b-2a

"Let me get this straight, pastor," Joe says, with a glint in his eye. Joe enjoys a good argument, especially a theological one. He relishes his self-described role of "devil's advocate," which he claims helps to keep his friend, the pastor, "on her theological toes."

"Now," he continues, "you say that God loves us no matter what we do. So why does it matter what we do? God will love us anyway, right?"

"Quite right," responds the pastor, as Joe finishes his fourth beer of the evening and nods to the waitress to bring him another one.

"Okay," says Joe, "here's how I see it—if God loves us then God certainly won't let any of us perish or go to hell or whatever you want to call it. So it doesn't matter what I do here on earth; I'm going to heaven when I die."

"That's up to God," says the pastor, with a wink. "I certainly hope to see you there."

"I still don't see why it matters what I do, if God loves me no matter what I do."

As the waitress places Joe's beverage in front of him, the pastor asks casually, "How many of those are you planning to drink tonight?"

"Hey, I'm just getting started," says Joe. "I don't have to work tomorrow."

"Well," says the pastor, "God's going to love you whether you stop drinking right now or whether you polish off a dozen of those beers. But if you keep drinking, you're not going to feel so good tomorrow morning."

"Man," says Joe, changing the subject, "I sure could go for a large plate of chicken wings."

God created a world in which our actions have consequences. That's one of the reasons why it matters what we do in this world.

God wants us to be accountable with our lives because God loves us. God knows what's good for us. And God knows that our lives are better and more fulfilling when we account for our actions and decisions. God cares about us, about every detail of our lives, including the quality of our lives, not just in the world to come, but here and now. God cares about everyone, every detail of every life, and the quality of every life, here and in the world to come.

Does it matter how much Joe has to drink? On one level, maybe not. He can go home, take some antacid and aspirin, and sleep off his hangover. In a day or two, his life will continue on as it always has. And God will love him nonetheless. Of course, there is the possibility that Joe's drinking will impair his judgment. He might try to drive home after drinking too much—a decision that could radically change not only Joe's life, but also that of any occupant of any car that Joe happens to come upon tonight.

We often hear people say, "It doesn't matter what I do as long as it doesn't hurt anyone else." And yet because each one of our lives has an impact on so many other lives, because we all are interrelated, because as the proverb goes, "No one is an island," we are hard pressed to name any "victimless crimes." If we harm ourselves, we harm those who love us. And if any one of us dares believe that no one loves him or her, he or she is overlooking the One whose love for the whole world grows deeper every day. What we do matters.

But Joe would rather not think about all that. He orders a large plate of chicken wings and another beer.

⚊ Liberating Laws ⚊

I find my delight in your commandments, because I love them.

⟨⟩ *Psalm 119:47*

Many Christians find the words of the psalmist a bit puzzling. Much of the 119th Psalm is devoted to praising God's laws and thanking God for the commandments and precepts that guided the lives of the people of Israel. As Lutherans, we understand that the most important role of the law is to remind us of our own shortcomings—to drive us to the gospel. Because none of us can completely follow God's commandments, we are driven to the cross and the merciful arms of our Savior. We also understand that the law helps to maintain an ordered society and prevents our world from falling into a state of total chaos. We recognize the need for laws, even if we grumble when we "unfairly" get caught in a speed trap.

Yet the writer of the 119th Psalm does not rejoice in the law because it reveals to him his own sinfulness or because it serves as a basis for social order. "When I think of your ordinances from of old, I take comfort, O LORD" (Psalm 119:52). The psalmist expresses an intimate, almost sentimental yearning for God's laws because he recognizes that they are a reflection of God's love for him. Most curious are the psalmist's words, "I shall walk at liberty, for I have sought your precepts" (Psalm 119:45).

As Lutherans focused on a grace-centered theology, we tend to think of laws in a negative way: The law condemns us; the gospel forgives us. The law enslaves us; the gospel sets us free. Could there possibly be a sense in which the law can enable us to "walk at liberty" as the psalmist proclaims?

At a youth gathering at our church, one teenage girl expressed her profound gratitude to her parents. "They say I can't be around people who do drugs. They say I'll be grounded for the rest of my life if they ever find out I've been at a party where people are using. And so when somebody asks me if I want to do drugs, I just say, 'No. I can't because my parents would kill me if I did.' Well, they wouldn't actually kill me. But, like, I don't want to do drugs, and they give me an excuse not to, if you know what I mean."

We know what she means. There is a sense in which God's laws can be liberating, too. They free us to be all that God wants us to be. They help to hold us accountable and thereby make our lives better. Yes, we know that none of us always follows God's laws as we should. And God's laws do remind us of our shortcomings. Yet God does not give us the law merely to taunt us, solely to drive us to our knees and remind us what miserable failures we are. God gives us the law because God loves us. The law points us to the gospel and sets us free. Even if we can't always do so perfectly, God still wants us to "walk at liberty" and follow in paths where our Savior leads the way.

— The Whole Shebang —

From [Christ's] fullness we have all received, grace upon grace.

John 1:16

Many of us understand God's grace as something that comes to us as a way of "taking care of our eternal salvation." Like payment made on a house, we may think of God's grace as a "paid-in-full" note on our eternal home. We can wear the moniker "Christian" during this life, but the real value of the program comes at the end, at death. Then, standing before Jesus or St. Peter, we will be declared "admission paid" and ushered into the kingdom of heaven.

What if God's grace is not limited to our salvation in the world to come, but also touches every area of our lives here on earth? What if there is a "now" as well as a "not yet"? So, yes, Christ has purchased for us a spot in that mansion with many rooms. On top of that, God also throws in our lives, our time, our talents, our relationships, our possessions, and everything we see, hear, touch, taste, smell, and experience on this earth and beyond. Suddenly, grace isn't just a five-star accommodation for which we're destined after our journey here on earth is complete; it's first-class service on every step of the journey.

In Exodus, Moses asked God, "Show me your glory, I pray" (Exodus 33:18). God responded, "I will make all my goodness pass before you, and will proclaim before you the name, 'The LORD'; and I will be gracious to whom I will be gracious, and will show mercy on whom I will show mercy" (Exodus 33:19). God said that Moses could not see God's face—it would cause immediate death. Instead, Moses was allowed to see God's back. God's grace in our lives is a bit like that experience Moses had hiding in the cleft of the rock protected from death, but privy to the goodness of God. God's radical grace looks like that—all of God's goodness passing before us.

When God's grace encompasses our entire lives, our achievement-oriented, competitive world turns upside down. Most of us look at accountability in human terms. We ask, "So what does God expect of us?" We want to know the rules. Like a half-hearted student, we ask, "What's the least I can do and still pass?" It might even be nice to have a set number of service hours, like many confirmation students have, so we could be accountable about our accountability. We like concrete expectations and measurements. We appreciate the concept of tithing, because it gives us a number, a way to measure our progress. We want to know the boundaries—the ways we can mess up, sin, and get kicked out. We want to know the minimum requirements for the maximum rewards.

Martin Luther challenged this limited way of thinking in his Small Catechism. As he explained each of the Ten Commandments, he enlarged their scope to cover all aspects of our relationships with God and each other. For example, the fifth commandment, which prohibits killing, also became about "helping and befriending our neighbor in every necessity of life" (*Book of Concord*, p. 343). While most Christians can claim that they have never literally killed someone, few (if any) of us have done all that we can to attend to the needs of others. If we had, there would be a more equitable distribution of resources among the world's population and fewer deaths from starvation or lack of medical care.

Paul gives a framework for living a life that is wholly claimed by God's grace in his letter to the Colossians: "And whatever you do, in word or deed, do everything in the name of the Lord Jesus, giving thanks to God" (Colossians 3:17). God's grace turns our measurement-focused accountability upside down. In Jesus, the goodness of God has passed before us and redeemed the whole of our lives.

If all of life is a gift, then everything we have already belongs to God. We're not accountable for just ten percent of it. We're accountable for the whole shebang.

⌁ Pregnancy and Other Hot Topics ⌁

*Or do you not know that your body is a temple of the Holy Spirit
within you, which you have from God, and that you are not your own?
For you were bought with a price; therefore glorify God in your body.*

⌁ *1 Corinthians 6:19-20*

God claims our whole lives—bodies included. The incarnation,
the fact that in the person of Jesus, God became one with us in an
actual physical body, demonstrates that God values our human physical well-being. During his years on this earth, Jesus attended to the
bodily needs of people as well as their spiritual ones. When people
were hungry, Jesus fed them. When people were sick, Jesus healed
them. When people were anguished or frightened, Jesus calmed their
anxieties. Jesus also attended to his own physical needs. He ate when
he was hungry. He rested when he was tired.

God has claimed our bodies as well as our souls. We live not just
for our own pleasure, but also for the good of God and the community. When speaking of accountability, it always comes back to
these primary relationships. As Jesus said, everything centers upon
loving God completely and loving our neighbors as ourselves. (See
Mark 12:29-31.)

We find two images helpful as we consider how God holds us
accountable for both our own and others' physical well-being. The
first image comes from our own experience of having children.
When Rochelle was pregnant, she took meticulous care of her body.
She ate a rich variety of foods. She didn't drink alcohol or smoke or
use drugs, because she knew that these things would harm the baby.
She exercised and tried to get enough sleep. She did all that she
could to take care of the baby inside of the womb. In Paul's letter to
the Galatians, he wrote, "It is no longer I who live, but it is Christ
who lives in me" (Galatians 2:20a). As Christians, we are—in a
sense—pregnant with Christ. Christ lives inside of us. Christ is in

our hearts, in our souls, in our innermost beings. If we love Christ and want him to live healthily inside of us, we will live in such a way that honors Christ.

The second image also comes from Paul. He wrote, "Now you are the body of Christ and individually members of it" (1 Corinthians 12:27). Not only is each of us individually pregnant with Christ, corporately we form the body of Christ. We are the presence of Christ in the world. When we participate in behaviors that hurt ourselves, we weaken the body of Christ. When we participate in actions that lovingly care for ourselves, we strengthen the body of Christ.

The work of caring for our bodies is holy work. When we take the time to love ourselves, to eat well, and to exercise, we are doing God's holy work. When we avoid addictive substances and when we keep our bodies safe from abuse and violence, we are doing God's holy work. When we wear seatbelts and visit the doctor and rest each day, we are doing God's holy work. Self-care is holy work.

Yet if our focus is solely on ourselves, we are overlooking what it means to be part of Christ's body. We live in a society where it has become increasingly tempting to attend to our own physical needs while ignoring the suffering of others. We diet, work out at health clubs, whiten our teeth, and tuck our tummies while across the globe, and often in communities not far from our own, millions of people suffer from malnutrition, ravaging diseases such as AIDS, violence, and abuse. Paul wrote, "If one member suffers, all suffer together with it; if one member is honored, all rejoice together with it" (1 Corinthians 12:26). We are accountable not only for our own physical well-being; we are accountable also for the well-being of others, *all* others in this world.

As individual members of the body of Christ we need to consider the impact our own lifestyles have on the well-being of others. The writer of 1 John states it pointedly: "How does God's love abide in anyone who has the world's goods and sees a brother or sister in need and yet refuses help" (1 John 3:17)? Throughout the

Scriptures, God's people are held accountable for how they respond to the physical needs of others.

We are amazed at how often contemporary discussions of Christian accountability center on "hot topics" like abortion or sexuality. While these issues are no doubt important, the treatment they receive in Scripture is minimal compared to the Bible's "hottest topic"—caring for the poor. Much is made about the sexual immorality of Sodom, the city God held accountable for its sins, yet the prophet Ezekiel proclaims: "This was the guilt of your sister Sodom: she and her daughters had pride, excess of food, and prosperous ease, but did not aid the poor and needy" (Ezekiel 16:49).

God cares about our bodies—every person's body. And while God certainly cares about how we conduct ourselves sexually, it would appear from a survey of Scripture that God is more concerned that everyone be fed.

⤙ Judgment Day (Yikes!) ⤚

So then, each of us will be accountable to God.

⤞ *Romans 14:12*

For our entire lives, we two have been hearing about the day when we will stand before Jesus, accountable for what we've done and not done with our lives. This promise—or threat—can cause us to question or modify our behavior: "I sure wouldn't want to explain *this* to Jesus!" As teenagers, we both practiced rebellion with frequent glances over our shoulders, more worried about God's judgment than what our parents would say. Christian comedians joke about what it will be like to stand before Jesus and explain our conspicuous consumption—our sport utility vehicles and mini-mansions, our 20-ounce steaks and cases of beer.

One of the best-known descriptions of the judgment day appears in Matthew's Gospel. Jesus spoke about separating people much like a shepherd separates sheep and goats. He said, "Come, you that are blessed by my Father, inherit the kingdom prepared for you from the foundation of the world; for I was hungry and you gave me food, I was thirsty and you gave me something to drink, I was a stranger and you welcomed me, I was naked and you gave me clothing, I was sick and you took care of me, I was in prison and you visited me" (Matthew 25:34-36). Jesus' point is clear: Those who care for the needy in society care for him.

Earlier in Matthew's Gospel, Jesus stated that even what we say will be judged. He said, "I tell you, on the day of judgment you will have to give an account for every careless word you utter; for by your words you will be justified, and by your words you will be condemned" (Matthew 12:36-37). The judgment—the final accountability—comes down to the concrete ways we love our neighbors, both in word and deed.

When Paul exhorted the people of Rome to stop judging and despising one another, he wrote, "For we will all stand before the judgment seat of God . . . .So then, each of us will be accountable to God" (Romans 14:10b; 12). But Paul also made it clear that on judgment day, not one of us will be made right before God because of the laws we have followed. (See Romans 3:19-26.) To use Jesus' image of sheep and goats, not one of us is good enough to earn "sheep status" because of our own actions. We are sheep only because of what the Shepherd has done for us. (See John 10:14-15.) On judgment day every human, from Mother Teresa to Adolph Hitler, ultimately can rely only on the mercy of our gracious and loving God.

This does not mean that what we do is not important. It is. Our actions in this life reflect who we are as children of God. They reflect the accountability we have to God and to the human family. Our actions let people know that we follow Jesus; they speak Jesus to the world. As St. Francis is purported to have said, "Preach the gospel at all times. If necessary, use words."

We each will give an account for our words and actions at the end of our lives. The account we give will not change our status as sheep. It will not change our eternal destination. Yet our words and actions do make a difference in the realm of God here on earth. The work we do to love God and our neighbor changes these relationships and effects change in the world.

Many of us are not looking forward to judgment day. Yet there is a sense in which knowing that Christ will ultimately judge our words and deeds can grace our lives here and now. We once attended a retreat where the leader asked us each to make a list of the 25 people, possessions, or experiences that we value most in our lives. At the bottom of the list we were to sign our name; at the top of the list we were to write "Jesus."

Then the leader asked us to cross out each of the 25 items on our lists one by one, so that finally only one's own name and Jesus' name remained. "This is what happens when we die," the leader explained. "In this life there are many people, possessions, and experiences that we value. Most of them bring joy to our lives and ought to be truly treasured. Yet none of them will last forever. In the end, only Jesus will remain, and we will meet him face to face."

Judgment day reminds us that Christ is our future as well as our present. It helps us to keep life's daily trials, failures, and temptations in perspective. All that for which we shall be held accountable melts away in the all-consuming light of Christ. On judgment day everything we have ever said or done will matter, and yet none of it will matter as much as Christ's enduring love and mercy.

Questions for reflection and discussion

1. What were some of your childhood beliefs about good and evil, salvation and damnation?
2. What do you remember about your confirmation day? Or, what do you anticipate your confirmation day will be like?
3. What laws do you worry about keeping?
4. What are some of your fears about judgment day?
5. Why do you think the way you live your life does or doesn't matter?
6. What are some examples of how the way you live has an impact on the lives of others?
7. Share an experience of God's grace in your life.
8. What areas of your life still need to be claimed by God?
9. What does being accountable to God mean to you?

2

Our Abilities
Are Not Our Own

It's the end of another exciting basketball game. The star of the team stands next to the well-dressed interviewer who asks, "So what was the key to your success tonight?"

The star looks straight into the camera and with sweat dripping off his chin, declares, "Before I answer that question, I want to give thanks and praise to God and my Lord Jesus Christ, who saves me from my sins and gives me the ability to play basketball."

Christian athletes giving a testimony after a game might sound a bit cliché. Still, there is truth to what they say. All abilities come from God, and may be used for God's glory and the good of the community or for our own selfish purposes. In Jesus' parable of the talents (Matthew 25:14-30), which immediately precedes the final judgment of the nations (Matthew 25:31-46), our Savior makes it clear that we will be held accountable for that which God has entrusted to us. While this obviously includes our financial resources, possessions, and time, it also includes our abilities and passions, whether they are playing basketball, baking pies, solving algebra problems, or fixing refrigerators.

⌐ With You I Am Well Pleased ⌐

So whether we are at home or away, we make it our aim to please [God].

⌐ *2 Corinthians 5:9*

We suspect that one of the reasons God wants us to be accountable with our talents and abilities has to do with our self-esteem. When we use the gifts God has given us for positive purposes we generally feel positive about ourselves. We're contributing to the common good. Even if our contributions are not always acknowledged by others, most of us experience a sense of satisfaction when we exercise our talents. Still it's nice to know that others notice the good we do.

One day last year we dropped our son off at school. As he climbed out of the car, we left with our usual parting words, "Sam, we love you."

"I love you too, Mom and Dad," he mumbled. Then he stopped for a moment. "Mom? Dad?" he asked.

"Yes, Sam?"

"I know you love me. But are you happy with me?"

Sam's question surprised us. For years we have made a point of telling our children that we love them. That we love them unconditionally. That we will always love them, no matter what they do.

We believe that all children, indeed all people, need to know that they are unconditionally loved. And, as Lutherans, we believe that this is the promise God has given us in Baptism. God loves us. God will always love us, even if we turn away, and no matter how many times we may mess up.

God loves us always. But is God happy with us?

When Jesus was baptized, a voice from heaven proclaimed, "You are my Son, the Beloved; with you I am well pleased" (Mark 1:11). God loved Jesus. And God was happy with Jesus. Why wouldn't God be happy with Jesus? He was perfect.

The rest of us don't always fare so well. Is God always happy with us? Of course not, we say. How can God be happy with us when we fall so short of doing what we ought to do?

"Mom, Dad, are you happy with me?" As parents, we love our son. And yes, most of the time we are happy with him. He's smart, polite, talented, and generous. Every day we tell our son that we love him. Yet we probably haven't told him that we're happy with him enough. Like most parents, we tend to notice our children more often when they are doing something wrong than when they are doing something right.

Is God happy with us? Sometimes, certainly. When we are using our gifts and talents in positive, constructive ways, God is pleased with us.

Try inserting your name among those words God spoke to Jesus: "_____, you are my child, the beloved, with whom I am well pleased." If you are like us, you'll agree that it feels good to know that God is pleased with you. Unlike human parents, God sees *everything* we do. And while most of us might find that an uncomfortable thought, knowing how often we fail to live as we ought, it's important to remember that because God sees everything, God "catches" us when we're doing what is right, not just when we're doing something wrong. God knows and is pleased with us when we do what is right and good, and that is certainly a powerful motive for wanting to be accountable for our actions.

─ Learning from Our Losses ─

Now, discipline always seems painful rather than pleasant at the time, but later it yields the peaceful fruit of righteousness to those who have been trained by it.

⭐ *Hebrews 12:11*

Friends of ours are teaching their son, six-year-old Kyle, how to be a good loser. For better or for worse, he has inherited both his parents' competitive natures. Predictably, Kyle does not always respond well in situations where he does not emerge victorious. Because his gloating is easier to tolerate than his moping, his parents have been tempted to let him win games on occasion. When Mom or Dad makes a few intentionally foolish moves on the checkers board, everyone's life becomes more enjoyable—in the short run. In the long run, it doesn't do Kyle much good.

And so of late, Kyle has been losing his fair share of checkers games. At the end of each defeat, he receives a pat on the back from his parents, compliments on how well he played, and a few pointers on what he might have done differently.

"Good game, Kyle," they say.

"But it wasn't a good game. I didn't win," he used to reply.

Now he simply glares at his parents with a determined look that says, "I'm going to win next time." And no doubt one of these days, he will start winning more often than he loses. His game is certainly improving.

Spiritual gifts come from God, but they do not come completely packaged and ready to use. (Yet how we wish they did! "Gifts of God—No Work Necessary. Just add [baptismal] water and you'll be amazed at what you can do!") Gifts need to be nurtured. Upon learning the alphabet, a child can't read Shakespeare's plays from cover to cover. It takes time to learn how to read. When a person first gets a driver's permit, he or she doesn't jump in the car and drive directly to Disney World. It takes time to learn how to safely operate a car.

The gifted (that's all of us) need to be cajoled, coached, challenged, even enticed to fully develop the gifts they have been given by God. The apostle Paul recognized that we need the support of others in order to fully develop our spiritual gifts. He frequently encouraged Christians to "encourage one another." The young man Timothy was urged, "do not neglect the gift that is in you, . . . so that all may see your progress" (1 Timothy 4:14-15). Scripture verses such as these remind us that Christian accountability includes seeking to make the most of what we have been given. This involves the two lessons that our friends' son Kyle has been learning—how to be disciplined and how to lose.

The Greek word *mathatas* that is used to refer to Jesus' disciples in the New Testament means "to be disciplined" in its passive form. Discipline (which is best understood as being trained or instructed rather than being punished) allows us to develop our God-given talents to their fullest potential. Discipline involves learning from the examples and successes of others as well as learning from our own failures and mistakes.

In basketball, a team does not score with every shot it attempts. Many games have been won on the rebound. A player shoots and misses. A teammate grabs the rebound and shoots again. Sometimes it takes several rebounds and subsequent shots before the team scores. A few years ago, a popular commercial featured all-star basketball player Michael Jordan promoting Nike™ athletic shoes. Jordan mentioned the many shots he had missed in his career. In doing so, Jordan indicated that his success was the result of perseverance in the midst of failure. Paul conveyed a similar sentiment when he wrote, "I will boast all the more gladly of my weaknesses, so that the power of Christ may dwell in me" (2 Corinthians 12:9b). Jordan attributed his success to having persevered in the face of defeat; the apostle Paul recognized the Maker of heaven and earth as the one who brings victory out of our defeat—by God's grace, accountable Christians persevere as they learn from their losses.

— Unused Gifts —

Why do you boast as if it were not a gift?

⋙ *1 Corinthians 4:7b*

Like good stewards of the manifold grace of God, serve one another with whatever gift each of you has received.

⋙ *1 Peter 4:10*

This is a story about two extremely talented people who refused to sing. One of them is a man we knew in college. He was a dedicated Christian who earnestly sought to do what was right in every situation. One day the campus pastor overheard him playing his guitar and singing in a secluded room of the college chapel. Knowing this man wasn't shy, the pastor said to him, "You have a real musical gift. Perhaps you would share it with us at one of our worship services someday."

"Oh no, I shouldn't do that," the young man responded.

"Well, I don't want to make you do something you don't want to do," said the pastor. "Can I ask why you think you shouldn't play your guitar and sing at a service?"

"In high school I played and sang at a youth service in my home congregation," the young man responded. "Afterwards, people complimented me on my wonderful talent. I listened to all their compliments and began to feel very proud. I knew I shouldn't have, but I did. I'm afraid that if I play in another service, I'll start to feel proud again. And I know that's not right. So I think it's best that I not tempt myself."

We also knew a young woman, just 12 years old, who was a member of one of the first congregations we served. The girl's mother let us in on her daughter's secret: She had a tremendous singing voice. She even had won a district award at her school. "I'd love for her to sing in church," said her mother. "But I doubt that she will. The last time she sang at a school concert she made a few mistakes. Not that anybody noticed. Her voice sounded wonderful like it always does.

But she thought she sounded terrible. She's so self-critical. And now she says that she's done singing." No amount of pastoral or parental persuasion could inspire this young woman to say "Yes" to sharing her talent with the congregation.

Both of these individuals were so centered on themselves that they had overlooked the fact that when they were baptized Christ took hold of them and claimed them as his own. Our abilities come from God. If we feel proud about them, then we are being proud of the One who gave them to us. As the apostle Paul writes, "Let the one who boasts, boast in the Lord." (2 Corinthians 10:17). If we're critical of our abilities, if we think we're not "good enough," then we are being critical of the One who gave us our talents in the first place.

And so we wonder—in sharing their gifts, would the young man have felt excessively proud? Would the young woman have embarrassed herself and proven not up to the task? We'll never know since both of them refused to sing.

⚊ Perfect! ⚊

And let endurance have its full effect, so that you may be mature and complete, lacking in nothing.

☙ *James 1:4*

Our son Sam held his book bag behind his back.
"You can't look inside."
"Why?" Rochelle asked.
"I failed my spelling test."
"It's okay, Sam. I still love you. Let me see."
Sam handed over his book bag. Inside, crumpled in a ball, was his test. Rochelle smoothed it out. The score read "9/10."
"Nine out of ten! Sam, that's great! You didn't fail! It's nearly perfect."
"Ten out of ten is perfect," said Sam. "Nine out of ten is failing."
It's no wonder Sam feels this way. Consider the messages in the media. One night, plopped in front of the television with a bag of popcorn, we nearly gagged as we happened upon a show about being "hot." (Hint: It's not about fevers or global warming.) Young men and women paraded onto the stage in itsy-bitsy swimming suits and posed in front of a panel of judges. The judges entered a score and one of two neon signs lit up—HOT or NOT. The show works on elimination, so even almost-perfect bodies got rejected. Those of us with a little too much "handle" in our love-handles watch such things with a sense of failure. Like Sam, we know that even nine out of ten is failing in a world that seems to accept nothing less than perfection.

We live in a judgmental culture. The media tells us who and what are hot (and not). Friends and family, strangers and acquaintances provide us with unsolicited criticism. At school, at work, and even at home, there are standards by which we are "judged." Some would say the church is no help in this matter, either. Despite our theology focused on grace, Lutheran church members often tell us that they hear nothing but judgment from the church. Some hear it from other members.

Some hear it from the pulpit. Even Jesus said, "Be perfect, therefore, as your heavenly Father is perfect" (Matthew 5:48).

Jesus, however, wasn't speaking of "perfect" the way we understand it. He wasn't referring to "perfect ten" spelling tests or bodies. The dictionary definition of *perfect* does not simply mean "ideal"—it also means "complete." In the Greek, the word is *teleios*, which means "whole" or "fully developed." As Christians, we are whole because of what God has done for us in Jesus. In a sense, we do what we can with what we have, and God completes us or makes us whole.

God called several people in the Bible who were less than perfect for the important tasks God put before them. Most recruiters would have put them on the "Reject" pile with one or more comments stamped on their applications: Doesn't meet minimum requirements. Not qualified. Lacks leadership experience. Inappropriate age or physical abilities for demands of the position. Questionable character. Lacks commitment.

Truth to tell, many of those God called would have agreed with the recruiter's assessment! When God called the old and barren couple, Abraham and Sarah, they laughed in God's face at the prospect of becoming parents to a whole host of descendants. Moses, by his own account, was a "bumbler," not gifted at speech giving and leadership. David had a problem with sexual indiscretion. Jeremiah was a child. Mary was a frightened young girl. Peter denied Jesus. Thomas doubted. Still, each of these people were called to special purposes. Each of them said "Yes" to God and used their lives, minds, and bodies to serve. In the end, they were accountable to the One who called and gifted them.

God still calls people who seem surprising choices—like us. We are people who maybe "failed" a few spelling tests. We wouldn't qualify for "hot." People may even tell us what we're bad at more than they tell us what we're good at. Still, in spite of the judgment of others, God calls us. The "perfect" candidate or not, we have something to offer. God has made us whole. When we are living the life God has called us to live, then we are doing holy work; we are being accountable with our abilities. It matters not that others think of us as "hot" or "not."

⚊ Let Your Light Shine ⚊

For you are all children of light and children of the day . . . .

⪧ *1 Thessalonians 5:5*

After the funeral, Jerry's family gathered in the fellowship hall for lunch and conversation. Although everyone in the room had seen this day coming, an overwhelming sense of sadness touched those who had come to mourn. Jerry had died at the age of 43 from complications due to chronic drug abuse. For years Jerry had been losing a battle that also had claimed the life of his older brother. With his death, his family felt relief that Jerry's suffering was over mixed with a sense of disappointment and incompleteness.

"My brother had so much promise when he was young," recalled Jerry's sister. "Everybody liked him. He lit up a room when he smiled. Sometimes when he was older, you could still catch a glimmer of what he was really like. But then the addiction would take over and the real Jerry would fade away. Such a shame. Such a waste."

Jerry's sister's comments reminded us of Jesus' words from the Sermon on the Mount, words that are read at many baptisms: "You are the light of the world . . . .let your light shine before others, so that they may see your good works and give glory to your Father in heaven" (Matthew 5:14, 16). Like all of God's children, Jerry was gifted with the light of Christ.

Jesus' words in Matthew 5:14 are descriptive, not prescriptive. The one who described himself as "the light of the world" (John 8:12) asserts that we, his disciples, share in his light. Jesus does not command us to be light. He states that by virtue of belonging to him, we *are* light. Regardless of what we do with it, the light within us cannot be extinguished. Like Jerry, some Christians either choose or are unable to let their light shine in the ways that most glorify God, yet none of us ever ceases to have Christ's light within us.

The command we receive when we are baptized is to let the light "shine before others," or as Paul puts it, "Live as children of light" (Ephesians 5:8). Paul describes spiritual gifts in much the same way that both he and Jesus speak about light. God bestows gifts of the Spirit upon Christians "for the common good" (1 Corinthians 12:7). God is the source of all gifts. All Christians are gifted in one way or another. What we do with our gifts is up to us.

Paul recognizes that spiritual gifts may remain unused or be misused (see 1 Corinthians 14). He continuously exhorts Christians to use their God-given gifts for the benefit of the church (1 Corinthians 14:12) and not merely for themselves. Ultimately God bestows spiritual gifts "to equip the saints for the work of ministry, for building up the body of Christ" (Ephesians 4:12). As accountable Christians, God calls us to use our gifts to work together so that all might know Christ's love.

— The Things We Do for Love —

For God so loved the world that he gave his only Son, so that everyone who believes in him may not perish but may have eternal life.

⋆ *John 3:16*

In the end, it all comes down to love. Love is the final measure by which we shall all be held accountable. After describing spiritual gifts in his first letter to the Corinthians, Paul describes love as the ultimate gift in the oft-quoted Chapter 13. All other gifts, including faith, lack purpose if they are not accompanied by love. Even truth without love can be brutal.

Yet despite all the times it is mentioned in Scripture, and perhaps because of all the ways the word is misused in contemporary culture ("Don't you just *love* ice cream?"), the concept of love remains somewhat elusive. St. Paul describes love in terms of what it *is* as well as what it *isn't*. He writes that "love is patient; love is kind; love is not envious . . . It does not insist on its own way; it is not irritable or resentful" (1 Corinthians 13:4-5). Like Paul, we know love cannot be reduced to any one thing. We know, too, that it is more than mere sentiment or feelings. Love simply is. Love always will be.

Indeed, it is possible to love without feeling love. We doubt that Jesus, being fully human, had "loving feelings" for his tormenters as he died on the cross. Yet, being also fully divine, Jesus' actions throughout his crucifixion revealed the perfect act of love. The writer of 1 John reminds us that love is ultimately revealed in what we do, not by what we say. The writer encourages Christians to "love, not in word or speech, but in truth and action" (1 John 3:18).

Many have argued that we should think of love as a verb rather than a noun, for love is always active, seeking out the one who is loved. Yet love is more than a verb. It cannot be reduced to a series of actions or choices we make. There is a sense in which "we fall in love," or perhaps we should say, love "catches" us.

When we fall in love, we don't keep track of all the things that we do for our beloved. We don't count the money we spend. We don't keep a record of the times we forgive our beloved. We are accountable to the one we love, yet our accountability stops being about expectations and commandments and begins to be a joyful spontaneous expression. Accountability stops being something we do to receive praise, honor, or glory.

Since God is love (1 John 4:16), there always will be a sense in which love is beyond our complete comprehension. Still Jesus said, "Just as I have loved you, you also should love one another" (John 13:34). On another occasion he said, "Love your enemies and pray for those who persecute you" (Matthew 6:44). It all comes down to love. And in the end, those to whom God holds us accountable (enemies included) will know that we have loved them, not because of what we said or how we felt about them, but by our actions.

Questions for reflection and discussion

1. What good deeds would you like God to "catch" you doing?
2. What excuses are you making for not using some of your God-given abilities to their fullest potential?
3. How has failing helped you to become more disciplined and develop your God-given abilities?
4. How has perfectionism kept you from using your gifts?
5. Share an experience of having a mentor encourage you to use your abilities.
6. How might you encourage others to "let their lights shine"?
7. What have you done for love?
8. If you could do one thing this year with your God-given abilities, what would it be?

3

Our Time Is Not Our Own

A friend of ours had an opportunity to adopt a baby when she was forty-five. "I'm crazy, huh? I'll be sixty-three when this kid graduates from high school." A wise mentor said to her, "You'll be sixty-three in eighteen years anyway. So, why not say 'Yes' to the joys and sorrows of parenting a child along the way?"

Our time is not our own. Many of us would like to think it is. Some of us buy books on how to better manage our precious time. Others use fancy calendars and electronic gadgets to schedule or help manage time. As humans, we try with all of our might to control the time we have on this earth. We cannot. Our time on earth—long or short—is a gift from God. What we do with the time—that's our gift back to God.

⌁ Spending Time ⌁

I do not want to see you now just in passing, for I hope to spend some time with you, if the Lord permits.

⌁ *1 Corinthians 16:7*

Be careful then how you live, not as unwise people but as wise, making the most of the time . . . .

⌁ *Ephesians 5:15-16*

When our son started kindergarten, he used to long for a day off. He often asked, "Today, are we going to SPEND THE DAY?" "Spend the day" is Sam's phrase for family time. Mom and Dad don't run around trying to accomplish tasks, Sam doesn't do homework, his sister doesn't have a sitter—we simply spend the day together. Sam says it with great vigor and joy, like it is the best thing in the world. It usually is. When we spend the day, we usually honor what we really need instead of what we think we want or what others demand of us.

In our materially focused culture, we frequently equate time and money. We say, "My time *is* money." The same words often are used in discussing time and money. Books promote methods that will help us to "manage" or "save" both our time and our money. Yet, we cannot manage our time in quite the same way that we manage our money. We cannot hoard time or put it in a bank and save it for a rainy day. And while we may say we are "living on borrowed time" or "I'll lend you my time," we cannot borrow or lend time. Time must be spent—now, while we have it. To quote another common phrase, "There's no time like the present." Truthfully, there *is* no time like the present. *Now* is all that we have.

Every month, popular magazines feature articles on saving time— or more accurately, spending less time on a particular task so that you can spend more time doing something you'd rather be doing. From cleaning to calculating your taxes, the magazines promise to tell you how to do it quicker. A friend once told us how to save time washing dishes. Evidently, if you load the dishwasher in a certain way, it takes less time to unload. As we stood together at the sink, contemplating this theory, we wondered aloud, "Do we want to save time in the kitchen?" We decided that for this task at least, we didn't want to save time; we preferred to spend it. We like Sam's theory. Doing the dishes the slow way may take more time, but it's time during which we get something as well: time to think, time to talk, time to pray.

Of course, time, like money, can be spent wisely or foolishly. Time can be wasted. Who hasn't known the empty sensation of having wasted a lot of time doing something meaningless? Time misspent is gone forever.

The apostle Paul had his own phrase for spending time wisely—"making the most of the time" (see Colossians 4:5 and Ephesians 5:15-16). We need only look to Jesus to understand what this means. To use Sam's term, Jesus "spent his days." Whether he was eating with friends, teaching about the realm of God, healing people, or spending quiet time with God, Jesus made the most of his time on earth. He lived with purpose.

Jesus said, "Do not store up for yourselves treasures on earth . . . " (Matthew 6:19). He was speaking about material possessions—items that can rust or be stolen. Given the way Jesus lived his life, we doubt that Jesus wants us to treat time like it is a commodity to be managed and carved and saved and borrowed. He went on to say, "And can any of you by worrying add a single hour to your span of life" (Matthew 6:27)? The answer is, of course not. So trust God in every moment, and live with the recognition that every moment is a gift, entrusted to us by God.

Jesus' parable of the talents (Matthew 25:14-30) is frequently read as part of church stewardship events. In this parable, the master commends his servants who took what he had given them and invested it so that its value was multiplied. We like to expand the interpretation of this parable, referring to it as "the parable of time and talents," for there is a sense in which time spent wisely is time invested. When we choose to spend the evening playing with our children or attending a Bible study rather than watching television, we are investing our time in ways that will pay fruitful dividends. When we walk the long way home, taking time to pray, reflect on our lives, and observe the beauty that surrounds us, rather than "saving time" by hopping in the car and speeding off to our next destination, we are investing our time wisely.

Every moment counts, and we shall give an account for every moment. Even if our days on this earth are not as long as we'd like them to be, the way we spend our moments may continue to have an impact on this world long after we have left it.

— There's No Time Like the Present —

For a thousand years in [God's] sight are like yesterday when it is past . . .

    ☙ *Psalm 90:4*

"So do not worry about tomorrow, . . . "

    ☙ *Matthew 6:34*

Like most people, we too often find ourselves making verbal to-do lists during dinner, worrying about paying next week's bills while at the park with the children, and obsessing about something somebody said to us yesterday instead of listening to the person who is talking to us right now. Sometimes, it's difficult to be present in the moment, focused on the task at hand.

Nearly every argument with our children can be traced to this single difference between them and us—they live in the present and we tend to focus on either the future or the past. As they stand squarely in the midst of play, engaged in pretending that they are giant panda bears, we are trying to command them into the future, saying, "We have to get ready to go to the library, and then we have to weed the garden before dark." It takes great effort for us to pull Sam and Elly out of their present play and into our future-oriented schedule. They have the same amount of difficulty getting our attention. They want to pull us out of our anxiety over time already spent and worries about the future and bring us fully into their present. "Mommy! Daddy! Try this!" And when we do "try this" and make ourselves fully present, we're the better for it. The lessons that we have learned at their feet we take with us into the rest of our world.

Jesus was fully present with people, no matter who they were—temple priests, tax collectors, strangers, or children. Jesus was aware of even the slight touch of a woman in a crowd. (See Mark 5:21-34.) Unlike those people we've all met at parties, the ones who while talking with you are looking over your shoulder for the really important guest, Jesus gave his full attention. In the same way, we more fully experience Jesus' presence with us now when we allow ourselves to let go of past worries and future anxieties and engage in the gift of the present moment. Our past is forgiven. Our future is in God's hands. We are accountable for now.

― Time-Out ―

Remember the sabbath day, and keep it holy.

⟨⇰⟩ *Exodus 20:8*

One of the popular parenting techniques of the past couple decades has been the "time-out." Parents send out-of-control children, often shrieking and kicking, to a quiet corner for a five-minute breather. A therapist friend once told us that time-outs are really more for the parent than the child, an opportunity for the parent to refocus and come back to the child with more clarity about how to handle the situation. We've been to many church meetings at which we've thought that most of the adults, ourselves included, could use a time-out to refocus and gain new perspective on the task at hand. In a larger sense, we've realized how much better our lives are when we take regular, structured time out from the daily grind to refocus and renew ourselves spiritually and physically.

God rested on the seventh day (Genesis 2:2-3) and later commanded that we, too, rest on the seventh day (Exodus 20:8-11). Jesus himself made a practice of taking time away from the haste of daily ministry for being alone with God and the disciples. St. Mark wrote, "In the morning, while it was still very dark, [Jesus] got up and went out to a deserted place, and there he prayed" (Mark 1:35). (See also Mark 6:46; Matthew 14:23; Luke 4:42; 5:16.) As they journeyed, Jesus frequently took time out to teach the disciples (Mark 8:27-33; Mark 9:30-32; Mark 10:32-34). Jesus took some of the disciples with him to Gethsemane to pray (Mark 14:32-42 and parallels).

When Jesus visited Martha and Mary (Luke 10:38-42), Martha raced around the house, distracted by the tasks at hand. Mary sat at Jesus' feet and listened to his teaching. Martha complained about Mary's idleness. Jesus rebuked her, saying that Martha was too distracted, that Mary had chosen the better part. We have all played the part of Martha. And for good reason! People need to eat; the children need a home, clothes, and a good education; there is work that needs to be done—important work. Jesus understood that, too. Notice that Jesus did not criticize Martha's work. Jesus chastised Martha for worrying and being distracted. There is a time for working. There is also a time for sitting and resting in the words and presence of Jesus. That time is called sabbath.

The practice of sabbath for Christians can include anything from attending worship to taking a whole day away from the roles and responsibilities of regular daily life. We need to take time out *from* the rigors of everyday life. The break refreshes and renews us so that we can attend to the essential matters of each day.

We also need to take time out *for* something. We need time to connect to God. We need time to be present with those we love— our family and close friends. We need time to simply be and allow our hearts to dream and imagine. We need time to engage our senses in the wonders of this world, to stretch our bodies, and to experience new delights.

The ancient Israelites regarded God's command to observe a sabbath as a gift. As Christians, we also can see this commandment as a sign of God's grace and love for us. We don't need to oppress ourselves by worrying that God will ultimately hold us accountable for every Sunday we worked or slept in instead of attending worship. Yet when we come to the end of each day, to the end of each week, and finally to the end of our lives, if we have held ourselves accountable for taking some sabbath time, we will no doubt discover that our days, that our weeks, that our entire lives have been richly blessed by the One who never asks us to do something unless it's good for us; unless it's good for the whole world.

⟶ A Way of Life ⟵

Happy is everyone who fears the LORD, who walks in his ways.

⟨⟩ *Psalm 128:1*

We both like producing: books, cookies, a freshly mowed lawn. Yes, we enjoy the process of writing or baking cookies and the smell of the green grass as we cut it. But more than that, we like the end product. We like to cross items off of our long list of obligations. We like moving work from our "in box" to our "out box."

We're not alone. Ours is a product-oriented society. No boss wants to hear that you are a week late with a big project because you're having so much fun working on it! Teachers want papers turned in on time. Those who measure the financial health of the nation don't measure the Gross National *Process*; they measure the Gross National *Product*. We're a nation that measures products: hours worked, home runs hit, grades earned, degrees completed, money invested.

Our children have been powerful reminders about the importance of process. When Rochelle was pregnant with our second child, we were overwhelmingly focused on "product." We had a book and a baby due at about the same time. We had work deadlines. We needed to prepare a place for the baby to sleep in our cramped little house. Our to-do list stretched out over many pages.

Most importantly, we wanted the baby to be healthy. So, we had a genetic ultrasound at eleven weeks to be sure. Throughout a previous nine-week pregnancy, Rochelle had experienced an ultrasound or two a week—so we knew the ropes. We expected to see a peanut-shaped blob. But this was a genetic ultrasound—and the picture was quite detailed. We looked up at the monitor mounted on the ceiling and saw an image of the baby with her hand in her mouth and joy-fully kicking her legs. When we saw the distinct movements of that little one whom we had yet to meet, we experienced one of those moments of clarity about life. Elly was not biding her time, waiting for the big moment of birth. Nor was she working hard at growing, getting her "product" prepared for the big day. This, we thought, is what it means to be alive! This is what God intends for our journey here—to be joyfully present to the process of life.

In our culture, it's easy to believe that God blesses products and not processes. Many congregations celebrate how far they've come in terms of anniversaries, baptisms, and confirmations. That's why we both have always liked the ordinary days, the long "green season" between Holy Trinity Sunday and Christ the King Sunday, often called "ordinary time." The gospel lessons are usually about Jesus' daily ministry. The services remind us that God blesses the process as well as the product. God is as present to us and as proud of us in the midst of a task as at the end of it.

Many people measure Christian accountability in terms of product rather than process, too, the assumption being that ultimately what matters most is where we are in the end. In seminary we heard stories about people who were so concerned about the final products of their lives that they waited until they were dying to be baptized. That way they would die and meet Jesus in "a state of grace." They gave little consideration to how they spent their life prior to their "death bed conversion."

Scripture seems to say that God might actually be more concerned about process than product. "What does the LORD require of you," asks the prophet Micah, "but to do justice, and to love kindness, and to walk humbly with your God" (Micah 6:8)? And Jesus said, "If any want to become my followers, let them deny themselves and take up their cross daily and follow me" (Luke 9:23). Walking with God and taking up the cross daily describe the process of the Christian life, not the final product. In the book of Acts, the first followers of Jesus were described as people "who belonged to the Way" (Acts 9:2). This is an interesting term for Christians. The first believers were not described as people who belonged to the "Final Product" or the "End

Result." They belonged to the "Way." The Christian faith is a way of life. How we live is more important than what we accomplish. Of course, our salvation is ultimately not about what we accomplish, but what Christ does for us.

Lutherans sometimes use the theological term "sanctification" to refer to the work of the Holy Spirit within and among us. Sanctification is the process whereby we who have been "justified" or "saved" by Christ move closer to becoming what God wants us to be. It is not an easy process, and it is usually marked by as many setbacks as accomplishments. Justification, the work of Jesus, is about the "final product." That's already been taken care of. Our concern is the process. Are we "walking the walk" of faith? Are we saying "Yes" to God in each moment of our lives, in each opportunity God sends our way?

— It's All in the Timing —

For everything there is a season, and a time for every matter under heaven.

<⊰> *Ecclesiastes 3:1*

In the midst of a difficult time in our lives, a friend told us a story about a "Zen butcher." As she described it, the western butcher—harried by many customers—hacked quickly at frozen, uncut meat until he got the desired piece to come free. Bits of bone and ragged edges needed to be trimmed off. The Zen butcher took a different approach. He waited until the meat was thawed to the appropriate temperature. He looked at the meat, touched it, and sought the absolutely perfect place to cut. Then, with one hard slice with his knife, the piece of meat was cut. There were no bone bits or ragged edges.

Her point was about timing. The first butcher didn't wait for the right time or look for the appropriate angle. In his urgency, he just hacked away until the meat was cut. The second butcher took his time, looked for the right place to cut, and was able to accomplish the job more easily. In life, we are often like the first butcher. We try to make things work that don't. Like trying to fit the proverbial square peg into the round hole, we push at relationships and ministries and other situations trying to get what we think we want. We work fervently against the clock even though the timing is not quite right.

Jesus was much like the Zen butcher. He paid great attention to timing. Knowing his task, he did not rush right into Jerusalem. He waited. When Peter recognized that Jesus was the Messiah, Jesus asked that the disciples keep it to themselves. (See Mark 8:29-30.) According to John's Gospel, Jesus did not want to go about in Judea because "the Jews were looking for an opportunity to kill him" (John 7:1). Jesus said, "Go to the festival yourselves. I am not going to this festival, for my time has not yet fully come" (John 7:8).

The Greek people used various words to indicate time. Two of the most popular were *chronos* and *kairos*. Each of these words had a unique meaning in the Greek language. The Greek word *chronos* referred to the continuous flow of time that can be measured by a clock and a calendar. The word *kairos* referred to a moment in the temporal process when something unique or special happened. When Herod wanted to know about Jesus' birth, he asked the Wise Men about the exact time when the star had appeared. The term here is *chronos*. (See Matthew 2:7.) In Mark's Gospel, when Jesus began his ministry, he said, "The time is fulfilled, and the kingdom of God has come near; repent, and believe in the good news" (Mark 1:15). The term here is *kairos*, suggesting a God-moment, a portion in history when the "timing" is right. In a sense, *chronos* is about clock time and *kairos* is about God's time. When we speak about timing, we are thinking about "kairotic time."

Part of being accountable is recognizing that both our time and our timing is held in God's hands. We are not in control. Forcing things does not work. We have a friend who wants to get married. As he approaches forty, he feels more pressure to find a partner now. Sometimes he tries to make relationships work, even though his better judgment tells him they will not. Like the first butcher, he pushes away at the relationships until they are ragged. So far, the timing has not been right.

Yet as the writer of Ecclesiastes reminds us, "there is a season for everything" (Ecclesiastes 3:1). Jesus said, "Beware, keep alert, for you do not know when the time will come" (Mark 13:33). Our responsibility is to be ever aware, ever open to the possibility that God's reign can come breaking into our lives at any time, often in unexpected ways. Jesus told a number of stories, including the parable of the faithful slave (Matthew 24:45-51) and the parable of the ten bridesmaids (Matthew 25:1-13) that highlight the importance of timing and vigilance.

Another image we find helpful is the moso tree. The moso is a bamboo plant that grows in China and the Far East. After the moso is planted, nothing appears to happen. For up to five years, even under the most ideal conditions, there is no visible growth. Suddenly, when the time is right, the tree grows nearly two and one-half feet per day, reaching a full height of ninety feet within six weeks. The moso tree can grow so fast because of the miles of roots it grew underground during its first five years of life. The image of the moso tree has been a helpful one for us as we try to live with God's sense of timing. When things don't go our way, we remember this tree, and imagine that we are growing miles and miles of roots underground that one day, in God's good time, will bear fruit.

— "Quantity Time" —

*This is the day that the L*ORD *has made; let us rejoice and be glad in it.*

⏤ *Psalm 118:24*

In these days when time seems to be in short supply, we've listened to a number of people talk about "quality time versus quantity time." These discussions often center around the amount of time we spend with our loved ones. Some have tried to argue that we don't need to spend as much time with those we love as long as the time we spend with them is "quality time."

The two of us, however, agree with a farmer who once told us, "Quality time versus quantity time is garbage. I can't give my crops quality time and hope they'll do okay. I have to be there for them, day after day, night after night. I take care of them all of the time." He's right. His crops need him day and night, not for just a few really quality hours when it works for him.

Relationships are built on time. Whether it's a relationship with God, one's children, a spouse, or friends, time matters. When people ask us how to raise spiritual children, we say, "Spend time with them." When we are asked about how to grow a healthy marriage, we say, "Spend time with each other." When people wonder how to grow in their faith, we say, "Spend time with God!"

Though the task appears simple, the accomplishing of it can be quite challenging. Our lives are packed to the brim with responsibilities and it's often hard to find time to spend with the people on whom we depend to "always be there." Even so, we cannot rely on quality time to be the bricks and mortar of a lasting relationship. It's time, and lots of it, that glues together our ties with those we love. Like the farmer and his crops, it's our availability that counts.

The thing is, quality time comes in the midst of quantity time. Sometimes quality time comes as a direct result of quantity time. It cannot be scripted or orchestrated. It happens spontaneously. Many "wanna be" writers talk about waiting to get inspired to write. They say, "I have this idea for a story. Some day when I get inspired I will sit down and write it." We've found that if we wait for inspiration, it never comes; we'd never write. As the saying goes, "Waiters wait and writers write." Inspiration comes to us within the process of sitting down each day to write, whether we feel like it or not.

It's the same in our prayer lives and in our relationships with others. If we waited to get inspired to pray, we wouldn't. Inspiration happens in the midst of daily showing up before God. With our children, quality time happens in the midst of long stretches of quantity time. We can never plan it. When we have tried to "sit down for a talk," it always falls apart. The real conversations happen when we're simply spending time together.

What this means is that every moment is sacred, pregnant with possibility. St. Paul recognized this when he wrote "pray without ceasing" (1 Thessalonians 5:17). Don't wait for the right time to pray. Now is the time.

Being accountable with time is not about counting hours or punching time clocks. For Christians, being accountable with time is about lavishly giving it away to those we love and even, at times, to those we can barely stand.

We build relationships when we spend time with each other. Play 100 games of Candyland™? Why not? Walk up and down the street holding hands with Grandma? Sure! Listen to our spouse tell that story again, laughing at all the right places? Of course. Pray every day for a lifetime? Yes! It's all about loving one another. And in the midst of this "quantity time," God breaks in and miracles happen: Our son shares a scary dream he had. Our stoic Grandma says thank you. Our spouse's eyes light up when we laugh. God answers our prayers in a way we never expected.

Questions for reflection and discussion

1. If you had a day to lavishly use time as you wish, what would you do?
2. What do you feel would qualify as spending time on the treasures of heaven?
3. Think about times when you were fully present. How did that affect your experience?
4. What might sabbath be like for you? Make a list of possibilities.
5. What are some of the ways you take time out for God? (Examples might include devotional reading, prayer walking, or Bible study.)
6. In your life, how have you seen quality time emerge from quantity time?
7. Share an experience of "kairotic" time.
8. Share an experience of trying to "force" things to happen when the timing was not right.
9. What are some of the important tasks in your life that you often put off until later?
10. What actions do you think God is calling you to take right now?
11. List the various areas of your life that consume your time. These may vary from individual to individual, but could include family, work, schools, friends, community, church, self-care, spiritual growth and sustenance, and so forth. With 1 being "seriously neglected" and 10 being "intentionally nurtured," assign a ranking to each area according to how well you feel you are being accountable with the time God gives you.

4

Our Possessions
Are Not Our Own

Eleanor spent a summer studying at a writer's colony on a scholarship, a scholarship she was shocked to discover that paid for everything—room, board, writing materials, even spending money. Upon her arrival at the writer's colony, she was handed a stack of money. Eleanor knew she had to budget it so that it would last. Still, she said, it felt odd to know that the money was a free gift. It was hers, and yet not her own. She had not earned it and yet she could spend it—in any way she wanted.

Eleanor's experience provides a good image for us as Christians. All that we have and all that we own comes to us from God. Even our ability to earn money is a gift. Our money and possessions are not our own. Like our time and talents, God entrusts these things to us in the hope that we will use them "for the common good."

— More Than Enough —

"... I came that they may have life and have it abundantly."

⌖ *John 10:10*

As a clergy couple, we enjoy any opportunity to worship together as a family. Recently, we attended a Sunday evening contemporary service at a church in our neighborhood. After worship, the pastor invited us downstairs for a simple supper of sandwiches, salad, and juice. He apologized to the table of guests, saying that they had not expected so many at worship. "I had to cut the sandwiches into thirds. Please take only one until everyone is served."

Our son looked with longing at the pile of sandwiches. Sam's eyes filled with tears as he asked, "Will there be enough for me?"

There was. We all ate our fill. As we cleared the dishes, we noticed that the sandwich plate was still full. What had appeared to be scarcely enough was more than enough to fill the bellies of the hungry crowd. The realm of God is like that. In Jesus' presence, scarcity is turned into abundance.

In the United States, the media, the retail industry, and other corporations make money by convincing consumers that happiness is found in the abundance of money and material possessions. They paint a convincing picture of scarcity coupled with their particular and spectacular solutions. Dingy teeth, messy closets, unhappy marriages, and spiritual emptiness have all become fodder for advertisers. The American consumer who watches television, reads newspapers and periodicals, or listens to the radio is sold a value system based on scarcity: "You do not have what you need to be happy" or "In order to be happy, you must buy this product."

The Bible presents another way of viewing life. From the beginning, the people of Israel understood God to be a faithful provider. God supplied Adam and Eve with enough food and shelter to live. God gave Abraham and Sarah a child and the promise of a nation.

When God called the people of Israel out of Egypt, God provided Moses as a leader to guide them. When the Israelites wandered in the wilderness, God provided food. God also made provision for the poor and the strangers: "When you reap the harvest of your land, you shall not reap to the very edges of your field, or gather the gleanings of your harvest; you shall leave them for the poor and for the alien: I am the LORD your God" (Leviticus 23:22). In addition, part of the tithe performed by the people of Israel was to be food set aside for the widows, orphans, and Levites. (See Deuteronomy 14:29 and 26:13.)

Aside from food and shelter, God gave abundant steadfast love to the people of Israel. In Psalm 136, the writer recounts God's deeds of love and mercy on behalf of humankind with the recurring phrase, "For God's steadfast love endures forever." The Hebrew word for "steadfast love," is *chesed* and suggests mercy.

Jesus continued this rich tradition of abundance. In his first miracle, he turned water into wine—and not just ordinary wine, but the very best! When Jesus fed the multitudes (John 6:1-15), he used a small boy's lunch to feed thousands. Though the disciples grumbled, seeing only limits and not possibilities, Jesus trusted that God would provide. All were fed.

In the Sermon on the Mount, Jesus instructed his hearers to leave behind the practice of worrying over food or clothing, because God would provide. Jesus used the birds of the air and the lilies of the field as examples of God's providence. (See Matthew 6:25-34.)

God loves and provides for us abundantly. We have nothing to worry about. For us, then, part of being accountable is letting go of our worry. It means refusing to buy into the "scarcity principle" espoused by advertisers. It means looking in our closets and pantries and saying, "I have enough." It means looking in the mirror and saying, "I am blessed." And it means looking beyond the confines of our homes and neighborhoods and deciding, "Out of what I have, what can I share?"

⟶ It All Depends on God ⟶

Trust in the LORD forever, for in the LORD GOD you have an everlasting rock.

⟨꙰⟩ *Isaiah 26:4*

In Jesus' life, trust was key. From Jesus' wandering and temptation in the wilderness to his prayers in the garden of Gethsemane, Satan tempted Jesus to take control of his own life and destiny. (See Luke 4:1-13 and Matthew 26:36-46.) But Jesus trusted God. He said "Yes" only to God. When Satan offered Jesus power, Jesus countered with the command to love and worship only God. (See Luke 4:8.) Jesus' relationship to God and his trust in his heavenly parent steadied him throughout his life on earth.

We experience similar temptations. Our culture's value system applauds those who get ahead on their own, who are "self-made" successes. Money, status, and possessions are seen as the keys to security and a sense of power and control in one's life. When our checking and/or savings account grows, it feels good to be able to say, "I did that." Having the money to purchase what we need and want lends a feeling of power. Providing food, housing, clothing, and extras for our loved ones gives us satisfaction. Even supporting the church and other charities can become a source of both pride and power.

We've heard people say that the happy medium between the American angst and full-out trust is this: "Work like it all depends on you, and pray like it all depends on God." It's a tempting theory: We get to hold onto a lot of control. We can keep our workaholic ways and still have a sense of control with our prayer lives. Perhaps a better adage would be, "In work, prayer, and life, it all depends on God."

Jesus challenges us to trust in the abundant providence of God. Accountability as it relates to money and possessions means focusing first on our relationship with God and trusting it. God has a history of being an abundant provider. As the Israelites wandered in the wilderness, God provided manna for them. God gave each enough for each day—no more, no less. Moses instructed the people to leave none over for the next day. But the people of Israel did not listen. They left it until morning and it became wormy and foul. Still, despite the anxiety of the Israelites, God provided this food for the forty years they wandered in the wilderness.

It's hard to imagine what putting trust in God for all that we have would look like. We think of our daughter who, at eighteen months, never worries about a thing. She wakes up each day confident that her loving parents will put food on her plate and fun in her path. She seeks blessings, love, and laughter in all that she encounters. She says "Hi" to everyone she meets, hoping for the best response. Whether she gets it or not, she wanders on with a cheerful "Bye."

We think, too, of our friend who works as a consultant and coach. He lives by his belief that God will provide all that he needs. He begins each day with a song that thanks God for the night before and the day ahead. He does not worry about who his next client will be or if there will be another. Instead, he focuses on building meaningful relationships with those he meets. From those relationships come his clients.

Another acquaintance of ours practices simplicity. She keeps only the possessions she absolutely needs. She gives away her extra possessions, with a prayer that they will be a blessing to others. She counts on acquiring those things she does need in a similar way, at rummage sales and discount shops or as gifts. Because of her lifestyle of simplicity, she is able to work less and devote more of her time to serving others.

～ Giving Back ～

[Jesus said,] "... Give, and it will be given to you. A good measure, pressed down, shaken together, running over, will be put into your lap; for the measure you give will be the measure you get back."

  Luke 6:38

"... For you reap whatever you sow."

  Galatians 6:7

"From everyone to whom much has been given, much will be required; and from the one to whom much has been entrusted, even more will be demanded."

  Luke 12:48

The biblical witness is clear about the importance of giving. What the Bible is not clear about is how much we are to give. Many Christians hold up tithing ten percent as the biblical ideal. Abram gave Melchizedek ten percent of all that he owned. (See Genesis 14:20.) Still, the biblical witness on tithing is confusing. The people of Israel were asked to set apart a tithe from their crops. With that tithe—either as goods or turned into money—they were to throw a big party in rejoicing and giving thanks to God for God's many blessings. The book of Deuteronomy says, "Spend the money for whatever you wish—oxen, sheep, wine, strong drink, or whatever you desire. And you shall eat there in the presence of the LORD your God, you and your household rejoicing together" (Deuteronomy 14:26). Every third year, the people were instructed to take their tithe to the town to be stored and then used to feed the Levites, resident aliens, orphans, and widows. (See Deuteronomy 14:28.)

The people of Israel were asked to give the "first fruits" of every harvest to the priest. (See Leviticus 23:9-14.) The priest would present the offering to God.

The concept of "stewardship" also comes from the Bible. A steward is a person who is given something to watch over for another. It does not belong to the steward, but the steward holds responsibility for it. A good example of "stewardship" can be found in a parable we have discussed before—Jesus' parable of the talents (Matthew 25:14-30). A man entrusted his property, in differing amounts, to his servants. Two servants were able to double the amount of talents. A third hid the talent, being afraid of losing it. Of course it is the first two who are rewarded—for they made good use of the talents while their master was gone. This text is often used to talk about how we give back our money and our time. It all belongs to God. We are not to hide it or hoard it, but to put it to good use.

So what are we to do? The Bible presents more than one way for us to give. We can tithe. We can offer our first fruits. We can try to be good stewards of our resources and give it all back to God. We can give cheerfully and abundantly! The point of the biblical witness is not to mandate a *how* but instead, to tell us *why* we give. It reminds us that we give to say thank you to God for all that we have received. We give because God has commanded (or Jesus taught) us to help those in need. We give so that others will see and know the good news of God's love. How we give and how much we give—that's up to us!

A friend of ours took a summer trip across the country by himself. Alan hoped to experience the joy of bountiful giving. He decided that whenever he ate in a restaurant, he would give each server a 100% tip. Whether Alan's meal cost $2.95 or $52.95, our friend tipped the whole cost of the meal. Waiters and waitresses ran out of restaurants holding bills in their hands, shouting to him:

"Wait! You left too much. You made a mistake!"

"That's no mistake," Alan responded. "It's a gift. Keep it."

When Alan returned, he said he learned that everything really is a gift—each day, each connection with another person, each meal. He felt that giving 100% taught him that it all belongs to God.

⁓ A Lesson Learned from Moving ⁓

For where your treasure is, there your heart will be also.

⪻ *Matthew 6:21*

Preparing for our recent move, we found packing to be extraordinarily difficult. With eight years' and four lifetimes' worth of stuff crammed into our old house, we had a lot to pack. Our wise neighbor said, "When I moved, I didn't pack anything that I would not be delighted to unpack in the new house." Her words became our mantra. As we sorted, we asked, "Will we be delighted to bring this object into the new house?" Large or little, it mattered not. We tried to take nothing with us that we did not want in our lives.

Of course we didn't always stick to our mantra. In the end, running out of time and patience, we modified the mantra: If we could not decide what to do with an item, we kept it. And in the end, our eyes so bleary with exhaustion that we feared we couldn't tell the difference between Grandma's china and the plates we had purchased at the dollar store, we packed everything.

Four months later, most of the stuff we moved into our new house sits untouched in the basement. We unpacked the basic necessities but nothing else. Living without fancy china, knick-knacks, wall hangings, and other treasures has been a freeing experience. In the old house, we spent much of our time "managing" stuff: dusting, cleaning, straightening, and protecting the precious treasures we'd collected or received. Now we have time and energy for more important things like playing and relating. One room, empty except for a chair, a bookshelf, and a stereo, has become our dancing room.

In a few months we will sort though the stuff in the basement, and will probably end up getting rid of most of it. Less stuff means less worry. Less stuff leaves open more room for new experiences and relationships.

Jesus spoke about not storing up treasures on earth. He warned that the treasures with which we fill our houses and garages can rust, wear out, and be stolen. In addition, these treasures take control of our lives. "For where your treasure is, there your heart will be also" (Matthew 6:21). Our hearts are the core of our very existence. The beating heart signals life. The heart is metaphorically the place where we hold passion and devotion. Jesus said that we cannot hold passion for both God and the treasures of this earth.

In one of the more troubling stories in the Gospels, a rich ruler came to Jesus and asked him what he must do to inherit eternal life. Jesus replied that although the man had faithfully kept the commandments throughout his life, he still lacked one thing. Jesus told him, "Sell all that you own and distribute the money to the poor, and you will have treasure in heaven; then come, follow me" (Luke 18:22). This story is especially troubling for those of us who are middle and upper class American Lutherans. First, because compared to the majority of the world's population, we are extremely rich. Second, because this text seems to imply that we can only be saved by our own actions—a belief Lutheran theology rejects.

Jesus goes on to say, "How hard it is for those who have wealth to enter the kingdom of God!" . . . Those who heard it said, "Then who can be saved?" (Jesus) replied, 'What is impossible for mortals is possible for God'" (Luke 18:14, 26-27). In other words, none of us, rich or poor, can do anything to save ourselves. We all depend on the mercy of God.

So does that let those with wealth off the hook? Hardly! The Bible repeatedly warns about the dangers of loving wealth more than God and reminds us that we will all be held accountable for our relationship with money.

It may be hard for many of us to read, "Sell all that you own," as a word of grace, yet in many ways it is. Less stuff means less worry. There's ample proof that contemporary Americans, who have more material possessions than any previous generation, experience no more life satisfaction than those who have lived with less. In fact, some would say we're more miserable. We are anxious about the debt we have accumulated to pay for our purchases. We worry that "thieves will break in and steal" all that we've acquired. And in the process we've allowed our love of possessions to replace our relationships with God and others. It all comes down to this—money cannot satisfy the way God satisfies. There is no replacement for loving relationships with others and with God.

God wants us to share not only because others will be blessed by it, but because sharing will bless us as well.

⤙ Keeping Accounts ⤚

Do not judge, so that you may not be judged.

⤞ *Matthew 7:1*

We went out to dinner with old friends. The bill arrived after a delightful, delicious meal. Our friend Joseph simultaneously grabbed for the bill and his calculator. Joseph began to assign food and numbers to each of us. He said to us, "Okay, you two had the grilled tuna, the steak, two salads, two sodas, and a fourth of the appetizer." Within minutes, the food, tax, and tips were accounted for as equitably as possible.

Ed and Tina, a young couple in their early thirties, keep careful account of the household chores. They each maintain a list of what has to be done and who does what. They take turns doing everything, including the baby's diapers. When they fight, they fight about who is doing more, who isn't; who gets time away from the home and kids, and who doesn't. It's been a long time since they did any of these chores out of love.

At church council one night, an argument broke out. Mrs. MacDonald, the church's treasurer, wanted to send a letter to everyone who hadn't given money in the last year. "It says in the constitution that those who don't give money or take Communion shouldn't be members. I have a list right here of 35 people who haven't given a penny. They shouldn't be members anymore." Mr. Marks, a retired man in his late seventies, stood up and spoke with emotion, "I know I'm on that list—me and the Mrs. We don't have money to give right now and it's hard. We try to do what we can around the church, helping out with yard work and in the office."

As humans, it's natural to want to keep account of what other people do and say, give and spend. Cain kept account of how God responded to Abel and for this reason Cain killed his brother. Joseph's brothers kept careful accounts of what Joseph received from their father and because of their father's generosity to Joseph, they sold Joseph to the Ishmaelites as a slave. The disciples worried over one another, wondering who was the greatest and hoping that Jesus would bless them with a special place in heaven. (See Mark 9:33-37; Mark 10:35-45.) In the parable of the Pharisee and the tax collector, Jesus spoke of the Pharisee who prayed in this way, "God, I thank you that I am not like other people: thieves, rogues, adulterers, or even like this tax collector. I fast twice a week; I give a tenth of all my income" (Luke 18:11-12). The Pharisee felt proud of who he was in comparison to others. When taking account of who had done what with their lives, the Pharisee found himself better than a whole host of people. Jesus praised the tax collector, though, who prayed only for himself, asking God to be merciful.

It's easier to keep account of the actions of others than to look at our own behavior. It's always possible to justify our own actions by saying, "At least I'm not as bad as that person." This is especially true when it comes to our attachment to material possessions. As Americans, it's easy for us to find someone who has more than we do. Our neighbor across the street has a nicer car, our brother has a larger home, our coworker just bought a home entertainment system that puts ours to shame. It's easy to lose sight of the fact that compared to the majority of this world's population we are wealthy beyond measure. We eat more than we need. We have more clothes than we need. We are constantly buying stuff that we don't need. Yet it's always possible to find someone who's more portly, better dressed, or has more gadgets than we do. "See, I'm not so bad," we say.

Christian accountability is not a competition. It's not about keeping score. It's about making use of the resources God has given us, and working with others who have also been blessed, for the good of all—for those with whom we share this world and those who will come after us.

⟶ Mrs. Newton's Gift ⟵

It is more blessed to give than to receive.

⟨❧⟩ *Acts 20:35*

Some of us give because we have to give. It is our nature to give. And even if God were not to hold us accountable for our giving, we still would have to give.

Her name was Mrs. Newton, and when Harold first met her she was 92 years old. He was a 26-year-old rookie pastor serving his first call in rural North Dakota. A lifelong member of the church, Mrs. Newton had become housebound and rarely left her three room apartment. On the first Tuesday of every month, Harold paid her a visit and served her Holy Communion.

Every month Mrs. Newton would say, "Now I know that Communion is God's free gift, but Pastor, I want to do something for you. Something to thank you for taking time to see me. So I baked you a cake."

Before Harold could say no, she would plop a slice of German chocolate cake down in front of him and insist that he eat it immediately. And then she would send him home with the rest of the cake and the instructions that he eat every last bite of it since "any fool could see" that he was much too skinny.

Every month Mrs. Newton made Harold a cake. One time when he made a rookie pastor's mistake and told her that she really didn't need to go to so much trouble, she set him straight. "Don't tell me what I need to do, Pastor. I need to make cake, and you need to eat it."

Their visits continued over a year and a half, and Harold started to notice as time went by that Mrs. Newton was becoming a bit weaker. She started to talk less. And sometimes when she placed his plate of cake on the table, her hand would shake uncontrollably. Then one month, for the first time ever, there was no cake.

"I'm sorry," she said. "I haven't felt like baking. My daughter brought over some cookies. Don't you leave without eating them. It's my little gift to you."

In the months that followed Harold ate cookies, and then potato chips and other snack items that tasted a little stale. Yet there was always something. Sometimes, Mrs. Newton's hands shook so much that Harold worried she might drop the plate.

One day he received a phone call from Mrs. Newton's daughter. "She's in the nursing home. We hated to do it. But she just can't live on her own anymore."

Harold stopped in to see her the next day. She had a nice room with a pleasant view, but he knew she wasn't happy. After he served her Communion, Mrs. Newton was at a loss about what to do. There was no plate to plop in front of the pastor, no cake, no cookies, not even a stale pretzel to munch on.

"Well, Pastor," she said. "I can't make anything for you any more. So I'll just have to say it. Thank you. Thank you for visiting me. You know how much it means to me."

And he did. Harold knew how much she needed to say thank you, and to give whatever she could. And so the last time he saw her, after she suffered a stroke and two days before she died, he knew exactly what she wanted to say to him. She couldn't speak then. But after he said a prayer for her, and after he placed a drop of wine to her parched lips, saying, "This is Christ's blood, shed for you," Mrs. Newton squeezed her pastor's hand. Just for a second. Just long enough to say all that she needed to say. Just long enough to give her pastor one final gift.

Questions for reflection and discussion

1. What do you need to trust God to provide for you?
2. Who are your role models for trusting in God? Why?

3. How has the media influenced your thinking about scarcity and abundance?

4. How have you experienced God's abundant provision for your life other than income?

5. With 1 being very low and 10 being extremely high, rank where your income level fits. Then, with 1 being low and 10 being high, rank how sufficient your income is in terms of being able to meet basic needs of food, shelter, health care, necessary transportation, and so forth. Given your financial situation, how are you able to give back a portion of what you've been given?

6. Return to your income ranking. If you are below the middle, imagine yourself being at "10." Given your experiences with financial need, how would you use this excess of income? If you are above the middle, imagine yourself being at "1." How would you cope if you had no place to live, couldn't get health care for yourself or your family, were often hungry, had no clothing appropriate for a job interview or transportation that would allow you to move into the workforce, and/or had no one to care for a young child or older relative if you did find employment? What kind of help would you want others to extend?

7. Do you feel the accumulation of wealth is sinful? Is it wrong to buy a luxurious house or car? To spend money on expensive art or world travel? To enjoy having more than is "sufficient"? Explain your feelings.

8. How important is getting rid of excess possessions? Explain your answer.

9. What stewardship practices have you found most helpful and why? (For example, tithing, pledging, "first fruits," and so forth.)

10. What are some of the ways you "give back" to God?

11. How have you been blessed by sharing with others?

5

This World Is Not Our Own
(We Share It with 6.3 Billion Other People)

Our neighbors are not always the people we would choose to be our neighbors. Jesus made this abundantly clear in his parable of the good Samaritan (Luke 10:29-37). Speaking to a group of Jews, Jesus tells a story of a man who is beaten and robbed along the road. A priest and a Levite both pass him by. The Samaritan, considered an outsider in the Jewish community, shows him mercy. Our neighbor is the person in need. Our neighbor is the one who helps us. Our neighbor is often not the person we'd expect or want to be connected to. This is the way it is in the realm of God.

∼ Think Globally, Act Locally ∼

[Jesus said,] "Whoever is faithful in a very little is faithful also in much; and whoever is dishonest in a very little is dishonest also in much."

✥ *Luke 16:10*

"Think Globally. Act Locally." This bumper sticker comes to mind every spring when we meet with confirmands. Visiting with them in their homes, we review the confirmation vows and ask them what these promises will mean in their lives. When we get to the part where they will promise, "to strive for justice and peace in all the world (*Lutheran Book of Worship*, p. 201)," we ask, "So, how do you expect to do that?" Silence. The teenager stares at the floor. "Any thoughts?" we prompt. After a few minutes, we talk together about the phrase, "Think globally, act locally."

Part of being accountable Christians, we tell them, is thinking globally. We encourage them to continue their journey of learning by seeking to understand what happens in the world. We also speak about how acting locally, even with seemingly insignificant actions, can "strive for justice and peace in all the world." Before we leave, the teenagers have a list of sorts. On it are the concrete ways they will serve Jesus and work for justice and peace in all the world. They include actions like learning about other countries, saying kind things to kids at school, singing in the choir, making sandwiches for the homeless, and greeting people at church. They are little acts of faithfulness that make a difference.

Perhaps that's what St. Francis had in mind when he penned the prayer about peace. It begins, "Lord, make us instruments of your peace. Where there is hatred, let us sow love; where there is injury, pardon" (*LBW*, p. 48). On it goes, with a whole host of concrete ways we can affect the world for good. We bring about change in our world with our small acts of kindness in our own homes and neighborhoods. Just as massive acts of evil begin with small acts, great acts of good begin with our daily gestures of kindness toward others. Acting locally can mean taking the time to talk to a neighbor, driving courteously, volunteering, or participating in interfaith discussion groups. Our little acts of kindness take root in the lives of others and bloom into more acts of love.

Each of these moments has the ability to change the world. Remember the infamous cartoon, where the boss yells at the man who shouts at his wife who punishes her child who kicks the dog? Acts of compassion and kindness can set off a chain of good behavior. The dog comforts the child who compliments his mom who kisses her husband who says something positive to his over-worked boss. The over-worked boss, who happens to work in the foreign relations department of a large company, passes these good feelings onto her colleagues in another country. And on it goes. Together these small acts help us to "strive for justice and peace in all the world."

— The Work of the Planet —

Be fruitful and multiply, and fill the earth and subdue it; and have dominion over the fish of the sea and over the birds of the air and over every living thing that moves upon the earth.

⊳ *Genesis 1:28*

The Psalmist wrote, "The earth is the LORD's and all that is in it, the world, and those who live in it; for he has founded it on the seas, and established it on the rivers" (Psalm 24:1-2). God has given us "dominion" over the earth and all that is in it. (See Genesis 1:26-31.) The earth belongs to God. We belong to God. God holds us all accountable for the care of the earth. In thinking about what this might look like, we have found several images to be helpful.

The first image came out of a conversation with our children. During the past year, we moved out of the suburbs and into the city. Immediately, we noticed the increase in human traffic. People walk more here. As a side effect, there's also more litter. We've taken to carrying grocery bags and gloves on our nightly walks, picking up litter as we stroll. Our son asked us why we have to do the picking up when we did not do the littering. We explained to him that it's similar to what happens at home. He helps pick up his sister's toys even though he didn't play with them. We wash his clothes even though we didn't wear them. Those tasks are the work of the family; the tasks we do because we are a family. This job—picking up litter—is *the work of the planet*—one of the tasks we do because we are part of the human family.

We live on this planet; its care has been entrusted to us. In this day and age, it's hard to think of ourselves as having dominion over anything but our tiny plot of land. This phrase, "having dominion," makes it clear that we along with the rest of the human family will be held accountable for the earth with which God has entrusted us.

The second image comes from the Bible. In several parables, Jesus uses the image of a house manager or a steward. (See Luke 12:41-48; Luke 16:1-13.) This is the person who is put in charge while the owner of the house is away. In a sense, this image gives us our job title. We are to be managers or stewards over the earth. This image empowers us. We are not mere household members, with no say and no impact over the house. We are managers. We are stewards. We make decisions. We are accountable for what happens on this earth.

The third image comes from Barbara Cooney's book *Miss Rumphius*. The book begins when Miss Rumphius is a small girl named Alice. Her grandfather charges her with this mission: "You must do something to make the world more beautiful." Alice fulfills her calling by planting flowers. When she walks, she carries lupine seeds in her pocket. Wherever she goes, she tosses seeds. The next spring, flowers bloom everywhere. The book ends with Miss Rumphius giving her niece the same commission she received from her grandfather, "You must do something to make the world more beautiful." To care for God's earth is to do more than maintain the status quo. Part of our task is to leave the places we have been more beautiful than when we found them. That may mean planting flowers, cleaning up polluted water, or freeing up vacant lots for use as city parks and gardens.

These three images have helped us to comprehend and to see as doable this overwhelming task—taking care of the earth. The images call us to accountability when life gets hectic and it would be easier not to recycle, not to pick up litter, not to think through the consequences of our actions. In those moments we remember that we have a job title, a job description, and a mission.

— Peace —

[Jesus said,] "Peace I leave with you; my peace I give to you. I do not give to you as the world gives. Do not let your hearts be troubled, and do not let them be afraid."

~ John 14:27

It's Thanksgiving. At two houses in the same town, families celebrate. For a moment, you are the proverbial mouse in the corner at each house.

At the first house, the large dining room table is laid with precision. Not a plate, glass, or fork is out of place. Grandparents, parents, and the grandchildren sit peacefully around the table. Polite conversation fills the air.

"Please pass the stuffing, dear."

"This is delicious."

"And what did you think of the game today, Son?"

"Splendid, Dad, just splendid."

The conversation continues in this way. No one talks about anything personal, political, or religious. Half the family votes Democrat and half votes Republican. Any conversation touching on anything family members feel strongly about has the potential of getting emotional and a little messy. One person at this table has just lost her job. The family knows, but doesn't want to embarrass her by speaking of it. A young couple has just lost a baby through miscarriage. No one knows quite what to say, so they say nothing. The young woman, still grief-stricken, eats with her head down, tears in her eyes. Afterward, many of the family members will say it was a "peaceful" holiday.

At the second house, the large dining room table is laid with care. Everyone has all of the right plates, glasses, and silverware—though little of it matches. The large family is gathered around the table. It's difficult to hear the snippets of conversation, as everyone is talking. They've covered a lot of territory in the past hour, over turkey and "tofurkey" (half of the family doesn't eat meat). So far they've argued over just war theory, drilling for oil in Alaska, social security, and world hunger. Now they sit, nursing glasses of wine or cups of coffee or juice, and catch up on each other's lives. One daughter is about to go to Guatemala with the Peace Corps. Her parents are upset about it; they worry about her. They argue a bit. They hear each other's point of view. In the end, no one's position has changed. But there has been change. They asked and they listened. As a result they now better understand—if only a little—why each person feels the way he or she does. From this, deeper understanding and change can grow. Afterward, the family members will say it was a "peaceful" holiday.

What does peace look like? Does it look like Thanksgiving at the home of the first family? For some people, peace is "peace at all costs," where people keep their opinions to themselves for fear of offending or hurting others. Peace is the absence of all conflict, emotions, and angst. For others, peace looks more like the Thanksgiving at the second home. Peace is dialogue that honors each person and hears each point of view. In this setting, peace is sometimes loud and rarely does everyone agree on anything. Sometimes people agree to disagree. But they don't close their minds or hearts.

What does peace look like? This has been a problem in the church from the very beginning. Paul wrote to the people of Corinth: "For it has been reported to me by Chloe's people that there are quarrels among you, my brothers and sisters. What I mean is that each of you says, 'I belong to Paul,' or 'I belong to Apollos,' or 'I belong to Cephas,' or 'I belong to Christ'" (1 Corinthians 1:11-12). Two thousand years later, we are still quarreling. More and more we hear about "conflicted churches."

Often, we want our churches to look like the first family, polite and kind and always getting along. We are afraid of a church that looks like the second family, arguing about many issues. It may not seem like the way things should be in church. What we end up with, unfortunately, is a church where people, afraid or unable to speak out in public, gossip and complain to other church members. Individuals bypass proper channels to complain about the pastor or other members. Extremely unhappy people bring these and other complaints to church meetings, sometimes shouting at clergy and council members. Pastors and parishioners leave the church, distressed, saying, "I never thought the church would be like this."

The church needs to wrestle with issues of peace and conflict and what a healthy community looks like. Peace at all costs is no peace at all. It may be easier on some level to avoid the important issues and play "nicety-nice" in public. Yet the individuals in such a community too often end up feeling hurt and alone, with nowhere to go for support and comfort. Important issues never get discussed. New ideas, creative innovations, and other changes are often met with resistance.

The second family provides a better example of what a peaceful community might look like. Peace is not the absence of conflict, but the presence of conflict expressed in a healthy way. In this community, consensus is not required. We do not all need to agree to be a community. Yet, each point of view is respected and valued, as is each member of the community. Dialogue is a frequent part of the community's time together. Everyone is invited to participate in the life of the community. Unpopular opinions are not held against people.

As Christians, accountable to both God and to one another, we need to think about what it means for us to be "at peace" with one another. As the church, God holds us accountable for sharing the message of Jesus Christ with the world. What kind of message are we sending? Those outside the church will no doubt judge us and the message of the gospel by how we Christians treat one another.

— Confession: Owning Up to Our Sins —

As it is written: "There is no one who is righteous, not even one . . . ."

⟨⟩ *Romans 3:10*

If we confess our sins, (God) who is faithful and just will forgive us our sins and cleanse us from all unrighteousness.

⟨⟩ *1 John 1:9*

Most pastors have heard a comment like the following: "Do you know what I like about the Lutheran Church? We don't have private confession."

Our standard response is, "Well, actually, Lutherans are not opposed to private confession. In fact, in the *Lutheran Book of Worship* we have an order for individual confession and forgiveness. (See *LBW*, p. 196.) If you're feeling particularly troubled by a sin you can make private confession to the pastor, who will forgive you in the name of Jesus and keep your confession confidential."

Okay, we'll be honest. We've been pastors for 15 years, and only on a few occasions has anyone approached us wanting to make a formal private confession. Oh, we've heard many confessions, but most of them come spewing out in the midst of informal conversation or counseling sessions. We find that most Lutherans prefer to keep their ritual confession on a corporate level.

Many Lutheran congregations begin their worship with an order for corporate confession and forgiveness. Knowing that God holds us accountable for unconfessed sin, we recognize the importance of admitting our shortcomings on a regular basis in the presence of God and one another. We also recognize that not one of us stands above the rest. "All have sinned and fall short of the glory of God" (Romans 3:23). "If we say we have no sin, we deceive ourselves . . . " (1 John 1:8). And so as a community of faith we confess that we who are "in bondage to sin" are also bonded by sin. We share a common fallen humanity.

The words that many Lutheran congregations use for corporate confession from *Lutheran Book of Worship* (pp. 56, 77, 98) are all-inclusive yet nonspecific. We confess that we have sinned "in thought, word, and deed, by what we have done and what we have left undone." As one of our parishioners observed, "That pretty much covers everything." In essence we are saying, "Forgive us all our sins, Lord, even those of which we might not be aware. Let nothing come between us and you, O God."

Most Lutherans seem comfortable with this kind of confession. As Lutheran pastors, we wonder what corporate confession might be like if each of the penitent was required to be a bit more specific about his or her sins. True, many Lutherans silently ponder their shortcomings during corporate confession. But what if we were required to publicly acknowledge and name our own individual sins in the company of our fellow believers? ("My name is John and this week I lied to my wife, wasted most of my time at work, and made some inappropriate comments about a driver who cut me off on the freeway.") We suspect that attendance at worship would fall off dramatically!

Yet we all benefit from searching our souls and examining our specific sins, both of commission and omission. We benefit from naming the wrongs we have done and the good we have failed to do, even if only in the silence of our hearts. When we allow ourselves to be held accountable for our sins (our very own sins) instead of hiding them behind a blanket confession, how much more does God's grace abound. Sin boldly! Confess your sins boldly! Own up to them. Be specific.

A friend of ours told of participating in a worship service as a chaplain in a prison. Before the service, the worship leader asked everyone to make a list of some of the most troubling sins they had committed during their lifetime. Since this was a congregation of inmates, some of the sins were quite heinous—armed robbery, assault, even murder. As part of the liturgy, the worship leader read from the list of transgressions, prefacing each one with the words,

"Lord, we confess that we have committed the sin of ____." The congregation responded, "Lord, forgive us this sin."

Our friend realized that by participating in this service, she and everyone present had confessed to some rather horrible crimes. Though she herself had never assaulted or murdered anyone, she was allowing herself to be held accountable for the sins of others. While her trespasses might have seemed petty in comparison to those of hardened criminals, she recognized that she shared a bond with these fellow Christians.

At the conclusion of the service the worship leader declared, "In the name of the Father, and the Son, and the Holy Spirit, your sins are forgiven."

Our friend said, "When I heard those words after confessing to such horrible crimes, I heard them in a new and powerful way. I heard them both individually and corporately. *You are forgiven.* You meaning 'me,' and you meaning 'we.' For the first time I realized how the woman described as a sinner in Luke's Gospel (Luke 7:36-50) must have felt when Jesus forgave her, and why Jesus said that those who have been forgiven much also love much. I gained a sense of what it must be like to be a murderer whose sins are forgiven."

We who are in bondage to sin, who are bonded by sin, share an even more powerful bond in our Savior, Jesus Christ, who "is the atoning sacrifice for our sins, and not for ours only but also for the sins of the whole world" (1 John 2:2).

⌒ What We Have Left Undone ⌒

[Jesus said,] "Truly I tell you, just as you did not do it to one of the least of these, you did not do it to me."

⪧ *Matthew 25:45*

We could have said something. But then the awkward moment passed and the opportunity was lost, much to our relief.

He was a friend of a friend, so we didn't know him all that well. We were talking with him about a variety of topics when the subject turned to race relations. We hadn't expected it, but suddenly the man told an offensive racist joke. He chuckled after telling it, and didn't seem to notice that we weren't laughing.

We glanced at each other, each of us wondering if the other would be courageous enough to tell this man that his joke was inappropriate and that we did not share his opinion about people of other races. Yet we both remained silent. And we both knew that our silence was terribly wrong.

We could try to justify the fact that we hadn't spoken up. We could say that he was a stubborn man, stuck in his ways, and that challenging his joke would only cause a needless confrontation. Our speaking up wouldn't change his ignorant opinions anyway, would it? We could say that we can't be held accountable for someone else's actions. After all, we weren't the ones who told the joke. We didn't even laugh at it.

Deep within us, though, we know that we bore the responsibility of our inaction. Call it a sin of omission. We had an opportunity to right a wrong, or at least to confront an evil (and there was no doubt that what the man said was evil, no matter how sincere or ignorant his intentions), and we failed to act. A quote often attributed to Edmund Burke, Irish philosopher and statesman, is: "The only thing necessary for the triumph of evil is for good men to do nothing." Burke lived in the 18th century, but the truth of those words is timeless.

We tend to think of accountability in individualistic terms, that we each shall be asked to answer for our own sins. And no doubt that is true. But what responsibility do we bear for the sins of others? We cannot control the actions of others. It would be wrong to say that the victim is as responsible for a crime as the one who committed it. But what about those who witness the crime, the passive bystanders who do nothing to prevent it?

We who have been baptized into Christ are intimately connected to our Christian brothers and sisters, but that is not our only community. We live in the world and cannot isolate ourselves from it. What we choose to do or not to do with our lives has an impact on more people than we might ever imagine, not only those in our family and immediate community, but also others around the world, even those of future generations. We may never know what damage has been done by our sins of omission—how someone's life might have been different had we taken the time to talk with him or her, or what changes a person might have made had we been courageous enough to confront.

The doctrine of original sin has been one way of understanding the common brokenness of humanity. " . . . Sin came into the world through one man, and death came through sin, and so death spread to all because all have sinned . . . " (Romans 5:12). Some who have written on the subject have linked our sinful nature to our sexuality or our bodies. Yet on a much more basic level, we can say that in Adam we all are one since in some respect we all bear responsibility for the brokenness of this world, not only because of what we have done but also because of what we have left undone.

Conversely, Jesus Christ has redeemed us not only by what he has done but also by what he has not left undone. In Christ, nothing that ought to be done remains uncompleted. In him all is complete "so that, just as sin exercised dominion in death, so grace might also exercise dominion through justification leading to eternal life through Jesus Christ our Lord" (Romans 5:21).

⟶ "You Also Must Forgive" ⟶

Put away from you all bitterness and wrath and anger and wrangling and slander, together with all malice, and be kind to one another, tenderhearted, forgiving one another, as God in Christ has forgiven you.

⟨⟩ *Ephesians 4:31-32*

A few years ago, just a few days before Christmas, a letter arrived in the mail addressed to "Nativity Lutheran Church" where Harold served as pastor. Inside was a money order for $100 made payable to Nativity Lutheran Church. It was accompanied by an unsigned note. "To whom it may concern," began the note. "Please receive this money and use it to do ministry at your church. I cannot tell you who I am, but several years ago, when I was a young man, a teenager, I was a member of your church. When I was a confirmation student, I would often steal money from the offering plate. I'm not sure why I did this, and I'm sure no one ever knew about it. For many years, I have felt guilty and sorry for stealing from the church. I always told myself that when I saved up enough money I would pay it back. I need to make up for the wrong I have done. Please forgive me."

Harold recognized this anonymous person's need to make restitution for the wrong he had done. On Christmas Eve, Harold shared the note with the congregation and made a public show of placing the money order in the offering plate.

The ancient Israelites also recognized the need for restitution and followed the process God had commanded to make amends after wronging another (Numbers 5:5-8). Restitution allows healing to occur both for the injured and the guilty party. As Lutherans we don't frequently talk about our need to make restitution, primarily because we recognize that nothing we do can fully make up for the wrongs we have done. Christ alone can pay the price for our sins, and that is already an accomplished fact, fully achieved through our Savior's death and resurrection.

Still, Jesus said, "So when you are offering your gift at the altar, if you remember that your brother or sister has something against you, leave your gift there before the altar and go; first be reconciled to your brother or sister, and then come and offer your gift" (Matthew 5:23-24). These words inspired the popular tradition of sharing the peace with one another before we approach the communion table. Jesus reminds us that when we have wronged another person, telling God that we are sorry does not fully solve the problem.

The act of making restitution and being reconciled with those against whom we have sinned strengthens the Christian community. Of course, reconciliation is a two-fold process. Jesus makes it clear that the one who has been wronged has an obligation even more urgent than that of the one who has sinned. "If another disciple sins, you must rebuke the offender, and if there is repentance, you must forgive. And if the same person sins against you seven times a day, and turns back to you seven times and says, 'I repent,' you must forgive" (Luke 17:3-4).

In fact, Jesus states that we will be held accountable for our refusal to forgive. We pray "forgive us our trespasses as we forgive those who trespass against us" because Jesus said, "For if you forgive others their trespasses, your heavenly Father will also forgive you; but if you do not forgive others, neither will your Father forgive your trespasses" (Matthew 6:14-15).

It's clear: Christians are obliged to forgive others. It may be the hardest thing that Jesus asks us to do. And yet, of course, Jesus never requires us to do something unless he himself first leads the way. Paul stated it succinctly when he wrote, " . . . Just as the Lord has forgiven you, so you also must forgive" (Colossians 3:13).

Ultimately, the Christian life centers not on being righteous, but on forgiveness. Being a Christian isn't about achieving individual perfection; it's about living in relationship. And so on that Christmas Eve, a few years ago, the people of Nativity Lutheran Church did something else after the pastor placed the anonymous man's restitution gift in the offering plate. In the prayers of the church they offered up a special petition: "O God, whoever this person is, wherever he is tonight, in obedience to the command of our Lord Jesus Christ, we forgive the sin your child has committed against us." Amen!

Questions for reflection and discussion

1. Give some examples of "thinking globally" and "acting locally."
2. What can you do to make the world more beautiful?
3. Share an experience of being in a healthy community. What was it like?
4. Make a list of rules for expressing conflict in a healthy way.
5. Share an experience of not speaking out when you felt you should have.
6. What do you find beneficial about confessing your sins in worship?
7. How has the experience of forgiving another person changed you?

6

Our Legacy Is Not Our Own

The one thing that would seem to be all our own is our legacy—what we leave behind. Like our financial estates, our mistakes and our successes must belong to us. We made them, after all!

But this is not the case! What we leave behind us, both at the end of the day and at the end of our lives, affects the whole community. Our actions, good and bad, faithful and rebellious, witness to Jesus' presence in our lives. They affect the daily lives of those we encounter, from the clerk at the grocery store to the people who live with us. Our sorrows and joys rub off on them in our interactions. A kind word can leave behind a legacy of generosity. In the same way, nasty words can contribute to a legacy of distrust.

Our legacy is our gift to the community. It consists of more than the estate we leave behind at the end of our lives. Our legacy is what we leave behind each day as a result of our actions and interactions in the world.

⌐ Living in Sin ⌐

For there is no distinction, since all have sinned and fall short of the glory of God.

⌐ *Romans 3:22b-23*

Awhile ago, we opened the newspaper to a headline that read, "Living in Sin." The article went on to discuss the Roman Catholic Church and its stance against divorced people who remarry. They are, according to the church, "living in sin."

"Aren't we all living in sin?" asked Rochelle. We laughed, remembering a time when that phrase was whispered between family members at the dinner table, as they gossiped about distant relatives who lived together without benefit of marriage. "Didn't you hear? She's living in sin."

We live in a sinful world. We all sin. Either we do the wrong thing or we fail to do the right thing or both. We are all living in sin. Because of Jesus, we all also are living in grace. Through Jesus' death and resurrection, we have been saved from the condemning power of our sin. Yet we still sin. We still need God's forgiveness. That's why we confess our sins on a regular basis. That's why we take time to pray the Lord's Prayer each day, "Forgive us our sins as we forgive those who sin against us." When we receive Communion, we do so remembering the one who died so that we might have pardon.

We are living in sin. It's important to remember that when we talk about Christian accountability. We may like to believe that we will be faithful all of the time. We won't. We will fail. Despite our efforts to do our best, we will sometimes do the wrong thing. No matter how good we get, we will continue to miss opportunities to be even better. We won't be able to do all that God asks of us.

As pastors we, like many others, have the kind of job where our work is never done. No matter how much we accomplish in a day, there is always something more we could have done. We could have checked on one more parishioner. We could have prepared more for our Sunday sermon. We could have started the paperwork for a new program. Still at the end of each day, we reach a point, sometimes out of sheer exhaustion, when we put down our work and rest for the evening. As pastors we know that we will be accountable to our parishioners and our colleagues for the work we have or haven't done. Yet somewhere along the line, we've also learned that we just cannot do it all.

We both like Martin Luther's explanations of the meaning of the Ten Commandments in his *Small Catechism* because of the way he expands the scope of the "Thou shall nots" to include what we ought to do as well as what we should avoid. And so Luther tells us that the commandment not to steal means more than refusing to take something that belongs to our neighbor. It also means that we should help our neighbors "to improve and protect their income and property" (*The Book of Concord*, p. 343). Luther's explanations help us to realize that God holds us accountable for much more than simply being good and following all the rules. They also remind us that none of us can ever do enough to fulfill the full scope of God's commands. Sure, we may not make a regular habit of stealing, but none of us has done all that we can to help our neighbors improve and protect their property. The world is not yet all that God wants it to be. There is still work to be done.

We *are* living in sin. We need God's grace to get us through each day. In Psalm 51, the traditional psalm of forgiveness, the psalmist asks God, "Create in me a clean heart, O God, and put a new and right spirit within me" (Psalm 51:10). In Psalm 103, the psalmist says that God moves our sins away from us, "as far as the east is from the west" (Psalm 103:12). There is a sense in these passages that through God's love and forgiveness, our slate is wiped clean. Yes, we are living in sin. We are also living in grace. Despite our failures, God loves us. Daily, hourly, minute by minute, we get the chance to begin anew. Thanks be to God!

— Future of Hope —

I pray that the God of our Lord Jesus Christ, the Father of glory, may give you a spirit of wisdom and revelation as you come to know him, so that, with the eyes of your heart enlightened, you may know what is the hope to which he has called you, what are the riches of his glorious inheritance among the saints.

Ephesians 1:17-18

The people of Israel were living in exile in Babylon. They had left behind their homes, their streets, their shops, and their land. The prophet Jeremiah told them to set down roots in this foreign country. He said, "Build houses and live in them; plant gardens and eat what they produce. Take wives and have sons and daughters; . . . multiply there, and do not decrease" (Jeremiah 29:5-6). Jeremiah told them that in seeking the welfare of the city in which they now lived, they would find their own welfare. He told them that in seventy years they would be brought back home. Seventy years! He went on to say, "For surely I know the plans I have for you, says the LORD, plans for your welfare and not for harm, to give you a future with hope" (Jeremiah 29:11).

God's word to the exiled people of Israel was one of hope and blessing. And yet, looking around themselves, hearing that some of them would die before getting home again, they must have felt hopeless. God's word to us is the same. No matter our circumstance, God promises to seek our welfare. God promises to give us a future with hope.

It's our task to detect this future. We have some ideas of the broad strokes of God's call. We know that we are called to love God and love our neighbors as ourselves. We know that Jesus has given us all a commission—to " . . . make disciples of all nations, baptizing them in the name of the Father and of the Son and of the Holy Spirit, and teaching them to obey everything that I have commanded you"

(Matthew 28:19-20). When we consider God's call, this is what we know for sure.

What we may not know, what we need to detect, is how each of us will accomplish this. How will we use our gifts and resources to praise God? How will our talents witness to God's redeeming love? How will our lives be signs of God's love for our neighbors in the world? We need to keep our eyes open for the signs God plants along the way. We need to listen to our own hearts. Through our gifts, our community, and our life experiences, we discover the future God has in mind for us.

In the Lutheran church, when an individual wants to become a pastor, she or he needs to experience an "external call." An external call is a call from the community of faith. The local congregation needs to recognize the individual's gifts for ministry and recommend them to the synod's candidacy committee and to the seminary. In the Quaker Church, when a member has an important decision to make, they may ask for a "clearness committee." This group spends three hours with the seeker, asking questions but never offering advice. It's an opportunity to wrestle with God's plans for one's life in the presence of the community of faith.

We all need to wrestle with God's plans for us. It's a part of what it means to be an accountable Christian. Most of us will spend our lives seeking God's help in discerning how to live our lives faithful both to our own gifts and to the community of faith. Having a vision is, in a sense, looking ahead at what we hope to look back on. It's planning what we would like our legacy to be. And that is why we wrestle with God over this. We know that God seeks our welfare. We know that God has planned for us a future with hope. With God's help and guidance, we hope to say "Yes" to living it!

Questions for reflection and discussion

1. How do you define legacy?
2. What are some of the things you wish to leave behind each day?

3. If your life on earth ended tomorrow, what would your *legacy* be?
4. Share an experience of proclaiming the gospel to another.
5. What are some ways that you have heard God's call?
6. Who are some of the people who have helped you to gain clarity about God's call?
7. How is thinking about one's legacy part of being an accountable Christian?

Bibliography

Brower, Michael and Warren Leon. 1999. *The Consumer's Guide to Effective Environmental Choices: Practical Advice from the Union of Concerned Scientists.* New York: Three Rivers Press.

Compolo, Tony. 1998. *Curing Affluenza* (Videocassette series: "Abundant life: What is it?"; "Money: How poor does Jesus want us to be?"; "Time: How much do I have to give away?"; "Stuff: How much can I have?"; "Support: What will help?"; "Next: What do I do come Monday morning?") Nashville: United Methodist Communications. Available at http://www.umcom.org/ecufilm.

deGraf, John, David Wann, Thomas H. Naylor. 2002. *Affluenza: The All-consuming Epidemic.* San Francisco: Berrett-Koehler.

deGraf, John and Vivia Boe (producers). 1997. *Affluenza: The All-Consuming Epidemic.* (Videocassette.) Seattle: KCTS-Seattle & Oregon Public Broadcasting. Available with study guide at http://www.pbs.org

deGraf, John and Vivia Boe (producers). 1998. *Affluenza: Simple Living and Its Rewards.* (Videocassette.) Seattle: KCTS-Seattle & Oregon Public Broadcasting. Available with study guide at http://www.pbs.org

DeGrote-Sorensen, Barbara and David Allan Sorensen. 2001. *Escaping the Family Time Trap: A Practical Guide for Over-Busy Families.* Minneapolis: Augsburg Books.

DeGrote-Sorensen, Barbara and David Allan Sorensen. 1994. *Six Weeks to a Simpler Lifestyle.* Minneapolis: Augsburg Books.

Dominguez, Joe and Vicki Robin. 1993. *Your Money or Your Life: Transforming Your Relationship with Money and Achieving Financial Independence.* New York: Penguin USA.

Melander, Rochelle and Harold Eppley. 1998. *Growing Together: Spiritual Exercises for Church Committees.* Minneapolis: Augsburg Books.

Melander, Rochelle and Harold Eppley. *Smart Choices: Making Your Way Through Life.* Minneapolis: Augsburg Fortress, 1998.

Melander, Rochelle and Harold Eppley. 2002. *The Spiritual Leader's Guide to Self-Care.* Bethesda, MD: The Alban Institute.

Miller, Arthur F. with William Hendricks. 1999. *Why You Can't Be Anything You Want to Be.* Grand Rapids, Mich.: Zondervan Publishing House.

OTHER LUTHERAN VOICES TITLES

Large-quantity purchases or custom editions of these books are available at a discount from the publisher. For more information, contact the sales department at Augsburg Fortress, Publishers, 1-800-328-4648, or write to: Sales Director, Augsburg Fortress, Publishers, P.O. Box 1209, Minneapolis, MN 55440-1209.

See www.lutheranvoices.com

Printed in the United States
123345LV00001B/58-69/P

9 780806 649993